Strategies for the Pro,

Becoming an Effective Peer Helper and Conflict Mediator

PEER POWER

BOOK ONE

FOURTH EDITION

Judith A. Tindall, Ph.D.

Routledge
Taylor & Francis Group
New York   London

Routledge
Taylor & Francis Group
270 Madison Avenue
New York, NY 10016

Routledge
Taylor & Francis Group
2 Park Square
Milton Park, Abingdon
Oxon OX14 4RN

© 2009 by Taylor & Francis Group, LLC
Routledge is an imprint of Taylor & Francis Group, an Informa business

Printed in the United States of America on acid-free paper
10 9 8 7 6 5 4 3 2 1

International Standard Book Number-13: 978-0-415-96231-5 (Softcover)

Library of Congress Cataloging-in-Publication Data

Tindall, Judith A., 1942-
    Peer power, book one : strategies for the professional leader : becoming an effective peer helper and conflict mediator / Judith A. Tindall. -- 4th ed.
        p. cm.
    Includes bibliographical references and index.
    ISBN 978-0-415-96231-5 (pbk. : alk. paper)
    1. Peer counseling--Problems, exercises, etc. I. Title.

BF637.C6T56 2009   Bk.1
158'.3--dc22

                                                                    2008020542

Visit the Taylor & Francis Web site at
http://www.taylorandfrancis.com

and the Routledge Web site at
http://www.routledge.com

MY JOURNEY IN THE PEER PROGRAMS FIELD

This book is designed to provide you with the guidelines you need as a trainer to teach others helping skills and communication skills based on the trainee book *Peer Power, Book One, Workbook: Becoming an Effective Peer Helper and Conflict Mediator.* If you need help in designing a program, please refer to *Peer Programs: An In-Depth Look at Peer Programs: Planning, Implementation, and Administration.*

Peer Power, Book One: Strategies for the Professional Leader is dedicated to all those trainers who have used my materials and given me feedback. This represents my own peer program journey over the last 40 years. My first peer-helping workbook was published in 1978. Obviously, it has been revised many times as a result of my own personal experience. I have witnessed the concepts and materials being used in a variety of settings, ages, cultures, and applications.

Those of you in schools have used these materials in setting up peer programs. Those of you in higher education, government-based institutions, and schools have helped refine and develop materials unique to your populations. Those of you in agencies, churches, and community programs have used these materials for setting up programs unique to your settings. Nursing homes have used some of the materials to develop unique programs for the elderly. Input from the United Nations Staff Outreach Support Program has helped refine the workplace as an ideal place for peer programs. Thank you for all of your input and creative ideas.

TABLE OF CONTENTS

INTRODUCTION

THE TRAINING PROGRAM

This training program is divided into three units. Unit A helps the peer program professional trainer and the trainee set the stage for developing basic skills and learning strategies to put a peer program into action.

For the trainees to be motivated to learn basic helping skills, they must first understand the program and have a baseline for their skills. They must be able to understand those who are different from themselves. It is essential for peer helpers to understand the whole concept of helping before actually starting the skills training. At this point, the group of trainees will feel a sense of unity and some bonding. The first unit, if the budget permits, is best taught in a retreat setting.

Unit B will focus on skills. Skills are to be introduced one at a time, with each new skill introduced to trainees only after they have practiced and become proficient in the preceding skill. Each skill is built on the previous skill(s) learned. Unit B may not have to be taught to all trainees. Many trainees will have mastered some of the basic skills previously. The professional leader will make a determination concerning the appropriate basic skills needed for your group. After completion of *Peer Power, Book One*, trainees are ready to undertake peer program projects. Selection of specific modules from *Peer Power, Book Two* may form the basics for advanced training. The design shown in Figure 1 should be followed exactly in introducing the skills. However, procedures for accomplishing goals can be created by each trainer to meet the needs of trainees.

Unit C will assist trainees when putting their skills into action. In order to put these basic skills into action, some work with knowing limits and confidentiality needs to be done. Another important consideration is teaching the trainees that

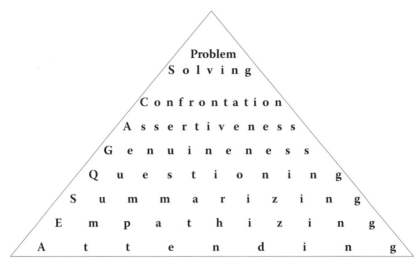

Figure I.1. Program design of eight basic communication skills.

they must take care of themselves first before helping others. Conflict mediation is often a natural strategy for peer helpers to implement both formally and informally. Peer helpers need a method for tracking their successes and challenges, and planning for their various activities. Unit C will assist the trainees in starting to put their skills into action.

As you begin to work with the peer helpers and their various service delivery activities, you will want to do additional training that can be found in *Peer Power, Book Two*.

TIMELINES OF THE TRAINING MODULES

An approximation of the amount of time that needs to be allotted for each module has been included to facilitate scheduling requirements for the entire training program. Modifications can be made in the suggested time schedule to facilitate the maximum growth of the trainees with whom one is working; however, with the first group of trainees, the recommendation is that one adhere to the suggested time schedule. Table I.1 is an outline of the schedule for the 10 training modules in *Peer Power, Book One, Workbook*.

TABLE I.1 SUGGESTED TIME NEEDED FOR TRAINING MODULES

Training module	Preparation	Group work
Module I	10–30 minutes	2–2½ hours
Module II	2–2½ hours	5½–6½ hours
Module III	10–30 minutes	2–3½ hours
Module IV	¾–1¼ hour	¾–1½ hour
Module V	1½–1¾ hour	2½–3½ hours
Module VI	2½–3½ hours	4¼–6½ hours
Module VII	1–1½ hour	¾–1¾ hour
Module VIII	0	1½–2½ hours
Module IX	0	2¼–3½ hours
Module X	1½–3½ hours	3–4½ hours
Module XI	¾–1½ hours	1½–2½ hours
Module XII	1½–2¾ hours	1½–2¾ hours
SD 1	1–1½ hour	2–3 hours
SD 2	30 minutes	1–2 hours
SD 3	35–90 minutes	3½–5½ hours
SD 4	30 minutes	3–4 hours

The total time requirement will depend upon several factors, such as ability and prior experience of trainees, time block for each training session, and opportunity for practice and preparation between training sessions. Because training conditions will vary from location to location, the training program is organized into modules with subdivisions (exercises) that can be taught individually or in combination.

The minimum time block for a training session is 30 minutes, with 45 to 75 minutes being preferable. At the start of each module in this book is an approximate time span for each exercise within the module. The overall approximate times by modules are provided in Table I.1. For planning the training program, suggested times can be used as guides rather than as absolutes. When exercises are grouped for being taught in the same module, the total time span probably will be less than when each exercise is taught separately.

PHYSICAL ARRANGEMENTS AND EQUIPMENT

The physical arrangements for a peer training program can be very simple or elaborate. The room must be large enough for practice to occur simultaneously in as many clusters as one third the enrollment in each training session. Ideally, it is important to have room for ice breakers and energizers. Acoustics are important because of the interaction desired among trainees during the training sessions.

A whiteboard is nice but not essential if a flip chart pad is available. The directions may be put on a focus machine for PowerPoint viewing.

Video and audio equipment for recording and playback are helpful for reinforcement and mobility. Trainees often benefit from viewing previously prepared recordings of skills being taught and of recordings made of themselves during role playing.

Furniture requirements are only a movable chair for each trainee, trainer, and visitor (if any). Generally, the chairs are arranged in a circle during times when trainees are together as a group and moved to smaller groupings as clusters of two to four are formed for interaction and role playing. Adult groups have used stationary chairs, but this is not ideal for interactive training.

Materials needed are *Peer Power, Book One, Workbook* and pen or pencil for each trainee. Each professional leader (trainer) will need *Peer Power, Book One* and materials for writing on the whiteboard or other means of capturing and summarizing ideas during discussions and presentations such as overhead projector or flip chart.

The professional leader should have read and completed *Peer Programs: An In-Depth Look at Peer Programs: Planning, Implementation, and Administration.* The CD that is a part of the book will help the professional leaders as they work with the program to begin, enhance, expand, and evaluate the program.

NUMBER AND AGE OF TRAINEES

The number of trainees in any given program is limited by the number of trainers, persons (potential trainees) available, facilities, and need for peer helpers once the training program is completed. A very minimum number at one time to facilitate the group interaction is suggested in many of the exercises. The maximum number with one peer helping professional probably would be 12, with 6 to 9 being more ideal. When the number of trainees exceeds 12, the suggestion is to have a second peer program professional if possible. Adult groups can be larger if there are other adults that help with the small group skill-building exercises. Large training groups are possible if you as the professional leader have trained other adults to work with the trainees and feel comfortable with large training groups.

Peer Power, Book One and *Peer Power, Book Two* have been used with both youths and adults. Older people often want to help others and often feel inadequate in skills needed to do so. Retirees can benefit as well as middle-aged persons or students in middle or high schools, higher education, training programs, and the military. Youth club members in organizations such as YMCAs, boys and girls clubs, churches, scouts, and farm groups often want to learn more about helping peers. No maximum age exists, and the minimum age is more dependent upon the person than the age; however, 12 to 13 is probably the generally accepted minimum for using this material. The reading and/or interest level of *Peer Power, Book One, Workbook* may be a factor to consider when selecting persons for a training program. Tindall and Salmon-White (1990) have developed a book for pre-adolescents utilizing similar peer helping training appropriate for that age.

FORMAT OF TRAINING SUGGESTIONS

Each module and exercise contains purposes, introductory information, training procedures in sequential order, and an application assignment for trainees between training sessions. The information supplied is above and beyond that supplied in *Peer Power, Book One, Workbook*. The peer program professional trainer will find the information supplements what trainees have in their workbook. The *Peer Power, Book One* series (consisting of two books—this book and the accompanying workbook) provides essential information and exercises for the total training program. The peer program professional will need to have both books, and each trainee will need to have *Peer Power, Book One, Workbook.* The trainer may also want to use audio and video equipment to demonstrate skills.

Unit A
SETTING THE STAGE

SETTING THE STAGE

As a peer program professional (trainer), it is important for you to do what you can to ensure that trainees feel comfortable with themselves and others in the group. As you know in any group work, the initial stages of forming and norming are critical for the group to be productive. This unit provides the framework to help your training group form, create roles, and set norms for the group. This unit will focus on exploring the trainee reasons for joining the group and getting a commitment to training and the peer helping roles they may want to deliver.

For a group to become productive, the trainees must first understand themselves, including their strengths and blindspots, and also others in the group. This will form a foundation that will allow trainees to help others who are different from them. As part of self-understanding, trainees must learn about their own assets and how to build them in others. Knowing their own values, heritage, and basic needs is also an important part of truly understanding themselves.

There are many different meanings of help within the whole field of helping. It is important that the trainees begin to understand helping as empowering others to help themselves. Therefore, Module III, which is on helping, is an important component of helping the trainees set the stage for helping others. Module IV will assist peer helpers in focusing on behaviors that stop communication.

Unit A, Setting the Stage, will provide motivation for the trainees to be ready to learn skills in Unit B.

MODULE I

WHAT IS PEER HELPING?

INTRODUCTION

This first module is devoted to explaining the program to the trainees and to others who may need to know what the program is about. A pretest is an integral part of the introduction module. Choose the appropriate pretest for the age of the trainees.

During the first group session, you may want to invite not only the potential trainees, but also others who may make significant differences in the trainees' attitude and behavior throughout the program. Important assets of the program are having all people know about the training program, what skills are to be learned, and the ways in which one can work with others after completing the program.

Goals

To learn about the training and the peer program

To pretest the trainees

To solicit their interest

To gain their commitment to participate as trainees

To help trainees get to know others in the training group

Time Needed—Trainees' preparation: 10 to 30 minutes
Group work: 2 to 3½ hours

Setup for Training

Have potential trainees sit in a circle. All others, such as observers, sit outside of the group.

Materials

- *Peer Power, Book One, Workbook* (one for each trainee)
- Pencil or pen for each trainee
- Name tag with name on shirt
- Sticky notes for trainees to utilize during training
- Snacks for trainees if budget permits
- Crayons
- Koosh balls or other things to hold in their hands
- Rewards to give to trainees at appropriate times (M&M's, smiley faces, gift cards (if budget permits), etc.)
- Tennis ball
- Colored dots
- Optional: CD player to play music and to bring people back from break

Training Procedures

1. Explain to trainees the purpose of the training program. At this point avoid lengthy details. Some of the purposes that need to be explained are:

   a. To learn about self

   b. To train individuals (peers) to help others (peers) with social, educational, emotional, and/or vocational concerns (you may want to be specific about roles in your program such as mentoring, tutoring, conflict mediation, etc.)

c. To learn the vision, mission, goals of the program. Give a one- or two-page handout about the program.

d. Answer questions that the trainees or others may have about the program.

e. To explain other roles for peer helpers. Refer trainees to material in Chapter 3, "Roles for Peer Helpers," in *Peer Power, Book One, Workbook*. Help trainees list examples of where and how peer helpers may assist their peers. Examples would include:

In schools:

- Helping new students adjust to school
- Helping during registration
- Helping tutor younger students
- Helping newcomers within the community to adjust
- Helping a peer find a social group or agency
- Helping with prevention programs
- Helping with at-risk youth
- Serving as rap leaders
- Serving as classroom presenters
- Serving as conflict mediators
- Helping provide service learning projects
- Serving as mentors
- Tutoring peers
- Serving as new student ambassadors
- Being youth listeners
- Standing as peer counselors
- Acting as 9th-grade advisory mentors
- Being crisis managers
- Participating in prevention theater
- Working as peer educators

- Working as peer facilitators
- Serving as leaders
- Working as health and safety educators
- Serving the community

In agencies:

- Helping in crisis centers
- Helping in orientation of new workers
- Helping in community outreach programs

In faith-based institutions:

- Helping in church school teaching
- Helping in leadership groups
- Helping in outreach programs
- Helping in peer ministry
- Helping with substance abuse
- Helping with family problems
- Helping with prevention
- Helping with health issues (AIDS, drugs, alcohol, smoking)
- Helping with wellness issues
- Helping to cover a telephone hotline
- Helping with safety issues

In the workplace:

- One-on-one helping
- Support group leaders

- Volunteers

- Group presenters

- Crisis managers

- Group health and safety educators

2. Answer all trainees' questions (parents of trainees less than 16 years of age are encouraged to attend this part of the meeting).

3. Begin building trust among trainees and set guidelines for confidentiality. The following points might be discussed:

   a. What is meant by confidentiality?

   b. What rights do individuals have concerning confidentiality?

   c. Why is trust important in a group being trained as listeners and helpers?

   d. What are the norms for such groups?

   e. Can trainees who are drug-free serve as role models?

4. Take a break and give the trainees a time limit to return; give out rewards for being on time. Set a timer so all will know when the break is over (optional: play music to bring them back from break). Ask others to leave the training program.

Evaluation Process

1. Determine how well those at this part of the training session understand the program by responding to all audience questions after goals and procedure for meeting those goals have been explained.

2. Analyze the pretest sheets (Exercise 1.1) and determine in part the skill levels of the potential trainees.

3. From Exercise 1.9, determine what reasons potential trainees have for taking the Peer Helping Training Program.

4. From Exercise 1.4 and 1.5, determine how well the trainees are able to interact with others in the group.

5. Exercises 1.6 and 1.7 will help you determine how well the trainees work in groups.

Measuring Outcomes

1. Establish that everyone in attendance at the opening session understands the goals of the program. You can accomplish this by answering all questions of trainees, parents, and others in attendance.

2. The extent to which the communication exercise is completed by trainees, including scoring, establishes the beginning levels of discrimination and communication skills of the trainees. Trainees' scores indicate their baseline skills. This could be used at the end of training to assess changes in skill level.

3. How well the trainees can state their reason(s) for participating will help the trainer know the level of commitment of the trainees and how the program can meet their needs.

4. How well the trainees interact with others, remember information, and seem to care about others will help the trainer know a baseline of listening ability and ability to care for others.

5. Observing how effective the trainees work in groups with specific roles is helpful in beginning to form the group and taking responsibility for group success.

EXERCISE 1.1
PRETESTING YOURSELF
COMMUNICATIONS EXERCISE

Goals

1. To gain insight into the personal interest of potential trainees

2. To understand their levels of competency

3. To gain insight as to the extent to which they might commit themselves to the training program

Time Needed—Trainees' preparation: no time required
Book work: 0 to 45 minutes

Assignments for Trainees Prior to Group Meeting

If you have met with each potential trainee individually and have had a chance to distribute the *Peer Power, Book One, Workbook*, then ask each trainee to read the first part of the book up to the pretest Exercise 1.1.

If the potential trainees have not read *Peer Power, Book One, Workbook* prior to the first group meeting, then no application would be indicated.

Introduction to the Exercise

The pretest will provide a means for you to assess each trainee's communication skills in terms of empathy based on discrimination and response. You can discuss items and trainees' answers with them after they complete the pretest. The same items will be used as a posttest at the end of the training program. Therefore, save the pretest sheets for comparison with posttest results later. Select the appropriate test.

Training Procedures

1. Have trainees open *Peer Power, Book One, Workbook* to Exercise 1.1 entitled "Pretesting Yourself: Communication Exercise." The purpose of the communication exercise is for the trainer to assess each trainee's skills in discrimination and response.

2. Refer to Exercise 1.1 in *Peer Power, Book One, Workbook* for explanation of directions and rating scale.

3. Use examples to help potential trainees better understand the rating scale. The following are examples you could use of conversations between a helpee and a helper together with an analysis of each of the helpers' responses:

Person	Response	Analysis
	High (H)	
Helpee:	"I'm having a problem with Betty."	
Helper:	"Betty is really upsetting you."	Heard the problem. Provided feedback. Responded to feelings. Helped person know feelings.
	Medium (M)	
Helpee:	"I'm not to blame, she is."	
Helper:	"Let's not talk about what she does."	Heard helpee. Encourages additional talk. Expresses willingness to listen.
	Low (L)	
Helpee:	"Yeah, she is always nagging me."	
Helper:	"What do you do to cause that?"	Not helpful. Makes helpee assume the blame.

4. Explain the rating scale as being based upon the degree of empathy in the response.

   a. Responses rated H included accurate paraphrase for both feeling and meaning of the helpee's statement.

   b. Responses rated M included accurate paraphrase for either feeling or meaning but not both.

   c. Responses rated L included neither accurate feeling nor meaning.

5. Ask the trainees to rate the responses for the first five statements, 1 through 5, in *Peer Power, Book One, Workbook* using L for Low, M for Medium, and H for High.

6. Discuss the responses for the first five statements. The response levels for Statements 1 through 5 that are generally accepted by experts are provided in Table 1.1.

TABLE 1.1 RESPONSE LEVELS ON PRETEST FOR YOUTH AND ADULTS

Youth			Adult		
Statement	Rating	Response	Statement	Rating	Response
1A	L	1a	1B	L	1a
	L	1b		L	1b
	M	1c		M	1c
	H	1d		H	1d
2A	L	2a	2B	L	2a
	H	2b		M	2b
	M	2c		H	2c
	L	2d			
3A	H	3a	3B	L	3a
	L	3b		H	3b
	M	3c		M	3c
	L	3d			
4A	L	4a	4B	L	4a
	H	4b		M	4b
	L	4c		H	4c
	L	4d			
5A	M	5a	5B	L	5a
	L	5b		M	5b
	H	5c		H	5c
	L	5d			

Optional: Omit the discussion and have the potential trainees proceed with Training Procedure #7.

7. Ask the trainees to proceed in the pretest with Statements 6 through 10. Ask them to write what they would consider to be a helpful response to the statement.

   a. In Statements 6 through 10, check each for an accurate empathetic response including feeling words and paraphrasing of the content. Use ratings L, M, and H as defined previously.

8. Have the trainees turn in to you the pretest sheets upon completion. The pretest will be readministered at the end of the training sessions as a posttest. You can compare the pre- and posttest results to determine behavioral changes in discrimination and communication skills.

9. Analyze the sheets from the pretest so as to establish a baseline for your training program.

10. Where necessary, talk with any individuals about whom the trainer is concerned in terms of readiness for the training program.

EXERCISE 1.2
NORMS FOR TRAINING

Goal

To help the potential trainees establish norms for their training time

Time Needed—Group work: 10 to 15 minutes

Introduction to the Exercise

It is very important at this point to get the trainees to discuss their norms for training. It is important that they bring up their own needs for successful learning as well as your needs for successful teaching.

Training Procedures

1. Discuss the need for norms in establishing a group. Give a few sample norms. (Examples: confidentiality, show care and concern, apply what you have learned, listen to others, participate, take responsibility for creating and maintaining a positive learning environment, keep phones and pagers on vibrate, take care of personal needs, relax, and have fun.)

2. Write on the flip chart additional norms that trainees may want. Draw upon answers they gave to Items 1 and 2 in *Peer Power, Book One, Workbook*, Exercise 1.2.

3. Make a list of what they discuss.

4. Try to develop a list upon which the group can agree.

5. Put the norms list on a large flip pad or other whiteboard to remain in view throughout training sessions.

Application for Trainees After the Group Meeting

Ask each trainee to review the list of norms they established so they will understand how the norms apply to him/her. Have trainees read Exercise 1.3 and complete it for the next meeting.

EXERCISE 1.3
CONTRACT FOR TRAINEES

Goal

To have trainees sign a contract for training

Time Needed—Trainees' preparation: 5 to 10 minutes
Group work: 10 to 15 minutes

Introduction to the Exercise

The trainees will sign a contract in which they agree to the training procedures and norms.

Training Procedures

1. Have them fill out a form for a training contract based on what was decided in Exercise 1.2.
2. Make sure that the contract fits within your work, school, and community guidelines.
3. Collect the training contracts and make a copy for the trainee or have the trainee write a second copy to keep.

Application for Trainees After the Group Meeting

Have each trainee prepare by reading Exercise 1.4.

EXERCISE 1.4
LEARN ABOUT OTHERS IN THE GROUP

Goal

To learn about people in the training group and practice listening skills and introductions

Time Needed—Depending on the size of the group
(six to eight)—not more than 30 minutes

Introduction to the Exercise

It is important to learn about people in the group that you do not already know and learn new things about people that you know. This exercise will help trainees practice listening and introducing skills.

Training Procedures

1. Pair trainees with a partner that they do not know or know well. Form a dyad.

2. Set a timer to give each listener a chance to ask questions: 4 minutes. Change roles, so the other person has a chance to ask questions. The listener may want to take notes or just try and remember.

3. Each dyad will introduce their partner to the whole group. The introducer will stand behind the person being introduced. They may want to put this in first person. Sometimes, this brings out interesting comments and dynamics. If trainees are too uncomfortable, simply have them state the name of the person and answer the questions.

4. When everyone has completed the introductions, have the trainees write out their responses to the questions.

5. Ask for volunteers to share their responses. Give rewards for sharing (stars, smiley faces, M&M's etc.).

Application for Trainees After the Group Meeting

1. Try to remember what others have said in the group.

2. Think about which group member you have the most "in common" with.

3. Think about others in the group that you would like to know more about.

EXERCISE 1.5
NAME GAME

Goal

To learn the name of others in the group (may be used as an energizer)

Time Needed—10 minutes

Introduction to the Exercise

Ask trainees to get into groups and have fun with this activity.

Training Procedures

1. If the group is large, get into a group of 8 to 12 people.

2. One person has a tennis ball. The person with the tennis ball tells his name and then tosses it to another person. The person has to repeat the name of who tossed them the ball and then state her name and toss it to someone else. Repeat until everyone in the group has stated their name and also stated another person's name.

3. At the end, ask a volunteer to please repeat everyone else's name (give them a reward, such as M&M's or a smiley face). Ask for other volunteers.

4. Discuss the following:

   a. What is the most challenging part of meeting new people?

b. How does learning and using people's names make you feel comfortable and welcome in a group?

c. How is it easier to work in a group if you know everyone's name?

Application for Trainees After the Group Meeting

1. Ask the trainees to think about the importance of knowing others' names.

2. Ask the trainees to think about how important it is for others to remember their name.

EXERCISE 1.6
GROUP ROLES

Goal

To learn how to work in a group and have a role in the group

Time Needed—15 minutes

Introduction to the Exercise

It is important to learn to work in groups and be responsible for the success of the group. This activity will help trainees learn about working in groups as a team.

Training Procedures

1. Divide into groups of four by counting off or giving people different colored dots.

2. Ask for one person to be the facilitator. If there are no volunteers, indicate that the person who is the tallest will serve as the facilitator. The facilitator appoints one person to be a recorder, one person to be a timekeeper, and one person to serve as an observer and also participate.

3. Each group will have one flip chart paper and a magic marker. The groups are to discuss what they hope to GET and what they hope to GIVE during the training (GET examples might be to learn new skills, learn how to mediate etc.; GIVE examples are listening, attention, cooperation etc.). Give the group about 5 to 10 minutes to work in groups.

4. The facilitator shares what the group shared with the total group. Put the sheet on the wall and refer to common examples of get and give.

5. Ask the observer in each group to share with their group: What went well? What could have gone better?

6. Debrief with the total group what they thought about the activity, what their feelings were, and how this applies to other parts of their life.

Application for Trainees After the Group Meeting

Think about issues in your community, school, and/or work that people face.

EXERCISE 1.7
PROBLEMS, PROBLEMS, PROBLEMS

Goal

To help the potential trainees identify the kind of problems they are faced with in their school, work, or community

Time Needed—Trainees' preparation: 5 to 10 minutes
Group work: 30 to 45 minutes

Introduction to the Exercise

In order to help trainees identify how their skills may be used, first identify the problem or problems that are prevalent at work, school, community, or home. The possible issues and problems might be drugs and alcohol, isolated people, low academic skills, and a variety of other examples.

Training Procedures

1. Have the trainee look at the two lists of problems in Exercise 1.7 and select the list most appropriate for his/her age.

2. Ask the trainees to add additional problems if they can.

3. Have them check the ones on their list that they believe are important.

4. Ask them to rank those items they checked as important.

5. Ask them to get into the same groups as in Exercise 1.6 and share their top three reasons for putting these into the top three. The group should come to consensus on at least six issues that face their school, workplace, and/or community. Write these issues on a flip chart sheet or whiteboard.

6. Have the facilitator of each group share the list with the total group.

7. Try to develop a consensus among the group about the top three problems. You may want to utilize voting if consensus is difficult. Have them use colored sticky dots or markers to mark the top three problems.

8. Lead a discussion about their top three rankings and what their reasons are for those rankings.

9. Have the trainees discuss how, in their roles as peer helpers, they might assist others in their peer helping roles with reducing these issues.

Application for Trainees After the Group Meeting

1. Ask the trainees to consider other kinds of problems with which they may want to use their skills.

2. Ask the trainees to study Exercise 1.8 and complete it for the next meeting.

EXERCISE 1.8
MY PEER HELPING ROLE

Goal

To help the trainees identify potential roles in which they may want to serve as a peer helper

Time Needed—Trainees' preparation: 5 to 10 minutes
Group work: 20 to 30 minutes

Training Procedures

1. Ask the trainees to look at the peer helper list in Chapter 3 and check one or more roles that they might want to perform as a peer helper.

2. Lead a discussion about the kind of roles that they would like to do.

3. Lead a discussion about the kind of skills that they already have in terms of one-on-one helping, small group helping, and large group helping.

4. Have them identify what skills and attitudes they already possess. To assist them, have them review the three examples provided in *Peer Power, Book One, Workbook.*

5. Have them add their skills to the list of examples, along with a peer helper role and setting where each skill might be used.

Application for Trainees After the Group Meeting

Ask the trainees to read Exercise 1.9.

EXERCISE 1.9
YOUR REASON FOR TRAINING

Goal

To learn the potential trainee's personal reasons for learning peer helping skills

Time Needed—Trainees' preparation: 5 to 10 minutes
Group work: 20 to 30 minutes

Introduction to the Exercise

Sharing the reasons for enrolling in the Peer Helping Training Program can help one understand the variety of motivations for joining the training group. The exercise is designed to have the potential trainees examine their own reasons and to share these with others.

Training Procedures

1. Make sure that each trainee has completed the three questions in Exercise 1.9.

2. Have the trainees discuss in the group meeting the answers they gave to the three questions.

3. Help the trainees gain a feel for what the training can do for them personally as well as in helping others.

4. Collect Exercise 1.9 sheets.

Application for Trainees After the Group Meeting

1. Ask trainees to read the introduction to Module II and complete Directions #1 and #2 in Exercise 2.1 before the next group meeting. Give rewards to those who have completed Exercise 2.1.

2. Ask trainees to make notes about their reactions to Module I. Ask for volunteers to share some of their notes.

UNDERSTANDING YOURSELF AND OTHERS

INTRODUCTION

In this module, you will model behaviors utilized in the initial stages of relating to others. Trainees will be able to initiate a relationship with the trainer and each other—persons with whom they will be working over an extended period.

As trainees talk with each other, you can help them sharpen their listening behavior. As they introduce each other, you will be able to analyze their listening behaviors, their willingness to talk in front of others, and other characteristics that will be useful in planning the balance of your training program.

Goals

To help trainees learn to know each other

To help trainees develop new listening behavior

To help trainees begin relating to others

To help trainees know their needs and helping values

To help trainees learn about their ASSETS and how to build ASSETS in others

To help trainees understand themselves through Type

To help trainees understand differences in others

To help trainees become aware of how to communicate with people who are different from themselves

To help trainees understand family, friends, and coworkers who are different

To help trainees become aware of their heritage

Time Needed—Trainees' preparation: 2 to 2½ hours for eight exercises
Group work: 5½ to 6½ hours for eight exercises

Materials

- *Peer Power, Book One, Workbook* (one for each trainee)
- Flip chart paper or whiteboard
- Pencil or pen for each trainee
- Name tag
- Sticky notes for trainees to utilize during training
- Snacks for trainees if budget permits
- Crayons
- Koosh balls or other things to hold in their hands
- Rewards to give to trainees at appropriate times (M&M's, smiley faces, etc.)
- Tennis ball
- Colored dots
- Optional: CD player to play music and to bring people back from break

Personality Types

Two effective ways to help trainees and yourself as trainer to know more about personality types are to take the Myers–Briggs Type Indicator (MBTI®) instrument and to have it interpreted after taking it. *To do so is not essential for using this module.* If the MBTI® tool is used, it needs to be done by a professional mental health worker who has received training and is certified to interpret the MBTI® tool. Once a person goes through a formal assessment (MBTI® or MBTI®-STEP II) or an informal assessment (Exercise 2.4), then the trainer can assist trainees in determining their individual "true type" or best fit. True type or best fit is what each trainee actually believes is his/her type.

If the formal assessment is not available, the material in this module will give you a framework that will enable you to obtain an informal determination of your own and other people's preferences in your training group.

A person's type, the combination of one's preferences from each of four scales, can be formally measured by two instruments, the MBTI® and the MBTI®-STEP II. Persons qualified to administer the MBTI® may order from Consulting Psychologist Press (CPP), 1055 Joaquin Rd., 2nd Floor, Mountain View, CA 94043, 800-624-1765, http://www.cpp.com. They also may order from the Center for Application of Psychological Type (CAPT), 2815 NW 13th St., Suite 401, Gainesville, FL 32609, 800-777-2278, http://www.capt.org. Both sources will provide a catalog of MBTI® materials and other related resources. The question booklets are reusable. There are three means of scoring the responses: by hand-scoring keys, by a computer-scoring service that provides each person with a printout of his/her type profile and an interpretation of it, or by self-scoring. Hand-scoring keys and computer scoring are available from both sources.

A necessary procedure is to help trainees understand their preferences and the preferences of others. By understanding one's type, trainees can move toward explaining differences in themselves and others. The concept of preferences will help trainees relate better to family and coworkers. Preferences also will help you be more effective in teaching trainees skills.

As a trainer, you can utilize preference information in teaching empathy, genuineness, confrontation, conflict mediation, and problem solving. Some points to know about each of the eight types are as follows:

1. **Extroverts (E)** have a more difficult time listening accurately to others.

2. **Introverts (I)** tend to need more time for processing and more time to respond.

3. **Sensing (S)** types will learn best if things are presented in a step-by-step manner.

4. **Intuitives (N)** will do better with an overview. They are not interested in specifics.

5. **Thinking (T)** types will have a difficult time learning to listen accurately for feelings.

6. **Feeling (F)** types will have a difficult time listening for meanings. They also have a difficult time with confrontation and conflict mediation.

7. **Judging (J)** types will do better with a structured learning environment.

8. **Perceiving (P)** types need an opportunity to be spontaneous and will do work at the last minute.

Training Procedures

1. Have the training in a room that is conducive to interaction among trainees and is large enough for trainees to move about freely. It should have movable chairs, sufficient heat and ventilation, and adequate lighting.

2. Be prepared to return exercise sheets and application sheets to trainees and, whenever possible, give written personal comments to each trainee.

Evaluation Process

1. You can determine the potential for a working group by the way trainees interact with one another during the training.

2. You can determine how engaged they are in building positive assets by the completion of Exercise 2.3, needs in Exercise 2.2, and helping values in Exercise 2.1.

3. You can determine self-understanding by trainees if they are able to identify all four preferences in themselves and internalize the type information as they use it with exercises in this module.

4. You can determine the understanding of communicating with others who are different from themselves by how well they do the communication exercises.

Measuring Outcomes

The outcome of Module II can probably be better determined at the next group meeting by having trainees at the beginning of the next training see if they remember their own type preferences and what they see in others.

One measure of outcome is whether or not every trainee knows their own assets and type as well as others' names and information about each of the other members of the group.

EXERCISE 2.1
HELPING VALUES

Goals

To help trainees identify helping values

To help trainees identify how this effects their lives

Time Needed—Trainees' preparation: 10 minutes
Group work: 20 to 30 minutes

Introduction to the Exercise

Values are often the basis for which people behave. It is important to help identify these values and to understand that these are the basis for making decisions.

Training Procedures

1. Ask the trainees to look at the possible values listed in their *Peer Power, Book One, Workbook* and then to list other values that they may have.

2. Ask them to rank these values.

3. Put the names of each of these values on newsprint and fasten all around the wall in the room.

4. Ask trainees to physically move to the value they ranked as 1. Ask them to discuss with their group exactly what that value means to them. Then ask them to move to the second value and then to the third value.

5. Bring them back together to discuss how it felt to see what other trainees' values are.

6. Ask them how these values guide their everyday living.

Application for Trainees After the Group Meeting

Have trainees prepare Exercise 2.2 by reading the directions for the next session.

EXERCISE 2.2
MY NEEDS

Goals

To help trainees understand Maslow's concept of human needs

To have trainees identify what their current needs are and what they believe their family's needs to be

Time Needed—Trainees' preparation: 10 to 15 minutes
Group work: 20 to 30 minutes

Training Procedures

1. Have them read material on needs if they have not already done so and discuss with them the meaning of the material.

2. Ask them to place an X on the chart where they believe their needs are and ask them to discuss this in the group.

3. Ask them what they believe their family's needs are.

4. Try to get them to explain where or how they believe their peer helping experiences will meet their needs (examples: love needs, esteem needs, self-actualization).

5. Read application assignments for Exercise 2.2 and give them feedback.

Application for Trainees After the Group Meeting

Ask trainees to write a pargraph explaining how peer helping will meet their specific needs. Ask them to study Exercise 2.3.

EXERCISE 2.3
ASSET BUILDING
(FOR YOUTH 14 TO 18)

Introduction to the Exercise

You may want to discuss how important it is to build assets as skills to reduce at-risk behaviors and build positive behaviors in the trainees and those they help. The at-risk behaviors and positive behaviors are available as downloads on the Search Institute Web site (http://www.search-institute.org).

Goals

To help trainees learn about the asset model

To learn what assets the trainees have

To help trainees learn how to help others build assets

Time Needed—Trainees' preparation: 30 minutes
Group work: 30 to 60 minutes

Training Procedures

1. Ask the trainees to review the list of internal and external assets and place a check on ones that they believe they have. Have the trainees ask others (friends and family) to see if they agree. This can be done as application before this exercise.

2. Ask the trainees to add the number of assets they believe they possess.

3. Help the trainees review what the Search Institute (http://www.search-institute.org) says about the power of assets. Lead a discussion to talk about whether or not they agree.

4. After the trainees review their list of assets, discuss if there are additional assets they would like to develop.

5. Ask them to think of one person they know well who they would like to help develop assets.

6. After completing introductions, discuss trainees' respones to the asset model.

Application for Trainees After the Group Meeting

1. Have trainees complete the checklists in Exercise 2.4 before the next meeting.

2. Ask trainees to think about how to apply the asset concepts in their daily lives.

EXERCISE 2.4
UNDERSTANDING MYSELF THROUGH TYPE

Goal

To help trainees learn about their preferences according to the MBTI® or other type material

Time Needed—Trainees' preparation: 10 to 30 minutes
Group work: 60 to 90 minutes

Introduction to the Exercise

This will help the trainees understand themselves and others. This exercise is the basis for other exercises in this module.

Training Procedures

1. If possible, please ask a counselor or psychologist to give the MBTI® or MBTI®-STEP II to trainees and give them individual feedback. If this is not possible, help them to determine their preferences through answering questions in Exercise 2.4. The idea is to help trainees determine their true type or best fit type.

2. Have them complete the list of eight questions, Item 2 in their workbooks.

3. If they are having a difficult time answering the questions, ask them to talk with a friend to help them determine their preferences.

4. Have them complete Item 3 in their books.

5. Have them complete Items 4 through 8 in their books. Circulate among them and offer assistance when appropriate.

6. Help each trainee develop a four-letter type.

7. Ask trainees to share their types with the group and have a discussion of the meaning of the experience to them.

8. Have them try to identify a family member or friend they know is different from themselves and then ask them to guess that person's preference.

9. Start a discussion about the impact of working and living with others who are different from them.

Application for Trainees After the Group Meeting

Have trainees study Exercise 2.5 and complete the first six directions before the next meeting.

Optional: If available, ask trainees to read *Please Understand Me II* by Keirsey and Bates (1998), *Type Talk at Work (Revised)* by Kroeger, Thuesen, and Rutledge (2002), or the *Introduction to Type* (1998) booklet by Myers.

EXERCISE 2.5
MY STRENGTHS AND BLIND SPOTS

Goal

To help trainees identify their strengths and blind spots based on type preferences

Time Needed—Trainees' preparation: 20 to 30 minutes
Group work: 30 to 45 minutes

Introduction to the Exercise

To help put the type material to work, it is helpful to have trainees apply the material to themselves.

Training Procedures

1. Ask trainees to look at their list of strengths and blind spots based on type theory.
2. Ask them to identify those that apply to them.
3. If the group is close enough, ask for feedback from others.
4. Have trainees do some of the work privately in their journal.
5. Have them identify strengths they would bring to a peer helping group. This concept is important to share so that all of the group will feel they are contributing to the program and that the program needs all types.
6. Discuss why different types are needed in the training group and when they apply helping skills.
7. Have trainees share what they have learned about themselves.

Application for Trainees After the Group Meeting

Ask trainees to study Exercise 2.6 before the next meeting.

EXERCISE 2.6
LEARNING HOW TO APPRECIATE
OTHERS WHO ARE DIFFERENT

Goal

To help trainees practice focusing on the concept that each person is different in terms of how he/she likes to be appreciated and motivated

Time Needed—Trainees' preparation: 0 to 5 minutes
Group work: 45 to 60 minutes

Introduction to the Exercise

To help people understand differences in people, it is important to know how to appreciate different types.

Training Procedures

1. Recognize that this experience can be very powerful to the group so you may want to post the newsprint lists that they develop on the wall and have them take notes.

2. Divide into preferences as directed in *Peer Power, Book One, Workbook*. You will probably have more Extraverts than Introverts and more Sensing than Intuitive types.

3. Repeat until each of the preferences has a newsprint sheet filled with ideas about how they like to be appreciated.

4. Divide them into pairs with different or somewhat different types paired.

   a. Ask them to role-play a compliment based on the other person's type.

   b. The person addressed then gives feedback concerning the compliment.

   c. Example: four-letter type, INTP and an ESTJ

An ESTJ says to an INTP, "It is obvious how much you have thought about this topic and how thorough your work is." The thinking type likes to be recognized for thoughts.

Application for Trainees After the Group Meeting

Ask each person to practice complimenting three other people using type ideas.

EXERCISE 2.7
COMMUNICATING WITH THOSE
DIFFERENT FROM YOU

Goal

To help trainees learn how to communicate with those of different types

Time Needed—Trainees' preparation: 15 to 20 minutes
                         Group work: 20 to 30 minutes

Introduction to the Exercise

This exercise will assist people in communicating with those who are different.

Training Procedure

1. Review the 16 types with the trainees. These 16 types are listed in *Peer Power, Book One, Workbook*.

2. Discuss Items 2 through 4 in their books.

3. Ask them to read about how different preferences like to be communicated with (Item 5, *Peer Power, Book One, Workbook*).

4. Ask them if they agree with things listed for the type they have identified for themselves.

5. Ask them to role-play one of the two situations with some-one who is different from themselves using things they have learned about that preference.

6. Ask each person to give feedback to his/her role-playing partner.

7. Process the activity.

    a. How difficult is it to talk with someone of a different type and make him/her understand a different point of view?

    b. What did they learn?

Application for Trainees After the Group Meeting

1. Ask trainees to identify a specific person (spouse, friend, etc.) who is different from them and practice selling them on an idea, activity, etc.

2. Have trainees study Exercise 2.8 and complete Training Procedure 1 before the next group meeting.

EXERCISE 2.8
KNOWING MY HERITAGE

Goal

To help trainees know their own backgrounds and see sim-ilarities of others

Time Needed—Trainees' preparation: 10 to 20 minutes
             Group work: 20 to 30 minutes

Introduction to the Exercise

It is helpful for trainees to get in touch with their own unique heritage.

Training Procedures

1. Have trainees draw a picture that would represent information about their heritage. (Example: If American Indian, draw a bow; if farmer, draw a farm implement; if family has a strong Christians faith, draw a cross, etc.)

2. Discuss questions in the student workbook.

3. Help trainees identify other cultures in the population with whom they may be working and discuss implications for peer helpers.

Application for Trainees After the Group Meeting

1. Have them talk with friends and/or coworkers to learn about other cultures and possible implications in working with people who are different from them.

2. Have trainees read the introduction to Module III.

3. Ask trainees to study Exercise 3.1.

4. Ask trainees to complete the notes section at the end of Module III.

5. Request one or two trainees to share their reaction to Module III.

MODULE

LET'S LOOK
AT HELPING

INTRODUCTION

In Module III, have trainees focus on helping by exploring helping behaviors in others and then in themselves. This can increase their concerns about which kinds of behavior are effective and which ones are ineffective.

Goals

To help trainees explore several different characteristics of helping behaviors

To help trainees identify ineffective helping behaviors that are used widely

To help trainees become aware of effective helping behaviors

Time Needed—Trainees' preparation: 1 to 1⅓ hours for six exercises
Group work: 2½ to 3½ hours for total module
Application: 1¼ to 1¾ hours for total module

Uses

Exercise 3.1 is best used with youth.

Exercise 3.2 may be helpful for adults.

Exercises 3.3, 3.4, 3.5, and 3.6 are useful for both youth and adults.

Materials

- *Peer Power, Book One, Workbook* (one for each trainee)
- Flip chart paper or whiteboard
- Pencil or pen for each trainee
- Name tag for name on shirt
- Sticky notes for trainees to utilize during training
- Snacks for trainees if budget permits
- Crayons
- Koosh balls or other things to hold in their hands
- Rewards to give to trainees at appropriate times (M&M's, smiley faces, etc.)
- Tennis ball
- Colored dots
- CD player and CD of soft music (for Exercise 3.2)

Training Procedures

1. Based on the time format for training sessions, decide how many sessions will be needed to teach Module III.

2. Review the training procedure steps for each exercise and prepare training format.

3. Collect the exercise sheets as each exercise is completed from Module II.

Evaluation Process

1. Evaluate the training during the sessions by input from trainees—the extent of interaction by all trainees, kinds of comments being made, whether or not exercise sheets are completed ahead of training session time, and the excitement (enthusiasm) with which trainees participate.

2. Determine whether or not trainees are moving toward creating a positive, healthy learning environment by the manner in which they discuss Exercises 3.3 and 3.4 (e.g., are they discussing behaviors or are they fearful of sharing with each other? Are they concerned with the topic of helping or are they more interested in themselves?).

Measuring Outcomes

The outcomes are to be measured in terms of the effectiveness of the training module in enabling trainees to identify and discriminate effective and ineffective helping behaviors by checking the appropriate qualities of their entries in *Peer Power, Book One, Workbook.*

EXERCISE 3.1
THE POWER OF PEERS

Goals

To help trainees become aware of the importance of peers and how they guide everyday behavior

To help trainees identify the impact peers have in both healthy and unhealthy ways

Time Needed—Trainees' preparation: 10 to 15 minutes for this exercise
Group work: 20 to 30 minutes

Introduction to the Exercise

This particular exercise can get trainees to think about the importance of peers in their lives currently and in their past. The real value has to do with helping them identify the unhealthy and healthy behaviors that their peers had and how these behaviors impacted the trainees.

Training Procedures

1. Ask each trainee to think about a peer who helped him/her get involved in some kind of unhealthy behavior. At this point it is very important for the leader to model what you are asking. (Example: A boyfriend that I had in high school introduced me to the world of drinking. I thought that was what grownups did so I did it, too, and that turned some of my high school friends against me.")

2. Have trainees discuss answers to Questions 1a through 1c listed under "Directions" in the workbook.

3. Ask each trainee to think about a peer who influenced him/her in a healthy manner. It is also important that the leader model this behavior. (Example: A girlfriend who was very confrontive made me feel angry and changed some of my behavior for the better by getting me into routine physical exercise.)

4. Have trainees discuss answers to Questions 2a through 2c in the workbook.

5. Have a discussion about the impact of peers.

Application for Trainees After the Group Meeting

1. Ask the trainees to consider peers who are currently influencing them and decide how the peers' influence affects them and the impact in terms of their behavior.

2. Ask them to turn in their application.

EXERCISE 3.2
IMAGINING MY HELPER

Goal

To help trainees understand better the behaviors of helpers

Time Needed—Trainees' preparation: 10 to 15 minutes for this
exercise
Group work: 20 to 30 minutes

Introduction to the Exercise

Trainees will be asked to try to imagine a particularly helpful person. To assist them, a useful procedure is to utilize some soft music in the background.

We often utilize imagery to help us understand the key components within ourselves; usually we have to become quiet for this to be effective.

Training Procedures

1. Ask trainees to sit very quietly, and close their eyes. Play some very soft music in the background and ask them to listen to the music for 3 to 5 minutes. As they do, lead them through the following relaxation exercise. Read very slowly.

   Get very quiet. Let your mind become quiet; let your body become quiet. Just think about relaxing every muscle and bone in your body. As you become more relaxed go back in time and think about when a friend, a parent, coworker, or relative was very helpful to you. Get that picture clearly in mind. (Pause.) Listen to what this person is saying and feel this person's presence. You might be an observer and see how the helper looked at you, what the behaviors were, how that felt, and in what way it helped you. (Pause.) As you are imagining the time with your helper, I would like for you to go and just sit there with your helper in the sun. Allow the warmth to surround both of you. When you are finished, I would like for you to open your eyes and feel refreshed and relaxed.

2. Ask each trainee to either write phrases or draw a picture that represents the helper.

3. Have them go to their *Peer Power, Book One, Workbook* and answer the following questions:

   a. How strong was the image?

   b. What behavior did they observe?

   c. How did it make them feel?

   d. What did they learn?

4. Make a list on a flip chart pad or whiteboard of characteristics seen in the imagery exercise.

5. Have trainees discuss characteristic behaviors of helpers.

Application for Trainees After the Group Meeting

1. Have each trainee develop a definition of helping.

2. Ask each to complete as much as possible of Exercise 3.3 before the next group meeting.

EXERCISE 3.3
EXPLORING HELPING BEHAVIORS IN OTHERS

Goal

To have the trainees become aware of helping behaviors that they like and dislike in others

Time Needed—Trainees' preparation: 25 to 30 minutes
Group work: 30 to 45 minutes

Introduction to the Exercise

This exercise is done best after the trainees have had time to identify individuals with whom they have enjoyed talking and sharing problems—after the trainees have completed Exercise 3.3. The group session is built around sharing those experiences and then extracting the positive and negative helping behaviors.

As a trainer, one can take an active role not only in getting trainees to share, but also in helping them identify helping behaviors. From the list that the group members make, you can assist them in extracting positive behaviors that they can practice.

To some extent, recording and discussing behaviors they don't like can be meaningful. Spend some time listing undesired (ineffective) helping behaviors and comparable ones to use instead. Often trainees need contrast (effective and ineffective) in order to remember better.

Training Procedures

1. Have trainees identify people with whom they talk about their problems. Identify by names, younger or older people, close friends or speaking acquaintances.

2. List the identified people on chalkboard, newsprint, or flip chart pad.

   a. Have trainees list verbal and nonverbal behaviors of those people trainees identified. Then have them give reasons for identifying each helpful behavior.

3. Have trainees brainstorm personal characteristics of the people whom the trainees find helpful.

4. Have trainees develop a definition of a helpful person.

5. Discuss how trainees presently help others.

6. List on chalkboard, newsprint, or flip chart pad the characteristics or behaviors that make the people (helpers) effective listeners.

7. Discuss effective helping behaviors.

   a. Attending behaviors of the trainee

   b. Effective listening behaviors of the trainee

    c. Responding behaviors of the trainee

    d. Initiative behaviors of the trainee

    e. Problem solving

8. List on whiteboard, newsprint, or flip chart pad character-istics or behaviors that the helpers had that the trainees did not like.

9. Help trainees identify behaviors to overcome or replace undesired (ineffective) behaviors.

10. Collect Exercise 3.3 sheets.

Application for Trainees After the Group Meeting

1. Ask trainees to practice helping behaviors they identified before the next training session.

2. If a time period exists between Exercise 3.3 and 3.4, ask the trainees to complete Exercise 3.4 before the next session.

EXERCISE 3.4
HOW DO I HELP?

Goals

To help trainees become better aware of helping characteris-tics they possess that others like

To help trainees recognize characteristics of behavior that are effective and those that are ineffective in helping others

Time Needed—Trainees' preparation: 10 to 20 minutes
Group work: 30 to 45 minutes

Introduction to the Exercise

After trainees have identified what they like in others who help them (Exercise 3.3), trainees generally enjoy practicing the behaviors during the next day or week as they help others. The practice enables them to transfer the list of behaviors from a "talk-about" to an action level. After trainees have experienced doing or attempting to do the behaviors, they often can verbalize better what they need in order to become the kind of person they would like to be.

Training Procedures

1. Have the trainees form clusters with three in a cluster.

2. Ask trainees to discuss in the cluster which desirable helping behaviors identified in Exercise 3.1 they were able to utilize in helping others.

3. Ask them to identify helping behaviors that were most meaningful as they used them.

4. Ask them to be prepared to share with the total group after 10 minutes.

5. After 10 minutes, regroup and have the trainees discuss what was gained in the clusters.

6. Use the whiteboard, newsprint, or flip pad to summarize what is presented, and then record the new list that they extract with your leadership.

7. Collect Exercise 3.4 sheets.

8. Return Exercise 3.3 sheets with written comments.

Optional: If no time existed between Exercises 3.3 and 3.4, then Exercise 3.3 sheets are to be returned when Exercise 3.4 sheets are completed.

EXERCISE 3.5
HELPING THROUGH SERVICE TO OTHERS

Goal

To help trainees understand that service to others is a way of helping

Time Needed—Trainees' preparation: none needed for this exercise
Group work: 15 to 20 minutes

Introduction to the Exercise

Service is an important aspect of our way of life. It is a means of helping others. By helping trainees to recognize different service jobs in the community and what those individuals do for others, trainees will be better able to understand how their peer helping will make a difference.

Training Procedures

1. Have trainees identify different service jobs in the community and list what those people do for others.

2. Have trainees think about some kind of service work they did in the past (i.e., helping an elderly neighbor by cleaning up his yard or working in the local animal shelter).

3. Ask about their reactions.

4. Help them process what they learned from that experience.

5. Brainstorm possible service efforts your group may want to take on.

Application for Trainees After the Group Meeting

Ask trainees to review Exercise 3.6 and come prepared to do the exercise during the group meeting.

EXERCISE 3.6
PRACTICE IN HELPING

Goals

To give trainees a helping experience early in the training without any evaluation

To help them provide feedback to each other

Time Needed—Trainees' preparation: no time needed for this exercise

Group work: 30 to 45 minutes

Introduction to the Exercise

Ask trainees to practice some helping skills. It is important for them to use the behaviors they have identified in Exercises 3.3 and 3.4. They need to try to use those behaviors.

Training Procedures

1. Have trainees divide into clusters of three.

2. In each group, ask them to discuss an issue for 2 to 3 minutes. Have one person present the issue, one person be the listener, and the third person give the listener feedback. Change roles until all members of the group have had an opportunity to play each role.

3. Discuss the experience.

Application for Trainees After the Group Meeting

1. Ask trainees to review Module IV.

2. Ask trainees to bring to the next meeting Exercise 4.1 sheets already completed.

3. Ask trainees to come prepared to do Exercise 4.2 during the next training session.

4. Ask the trainees to complete the note section at the end of the module and ask some to share their reactions.

MODULE **IV**

COMMUNICATION STOPPERS

INTRODUCTION

Communication stoppers are behaviors that, although they appear to be helpful, are really responses that are negative in effect and retard helpful interpersonal relationships. Helping the trainees recognize the communication stoppers and learn new behaviors to use in their place can be very meaningful. Eleven different kinds of communication stoppers are identified. Through illustrations of each kind, you will be able to help trainees increase their awareness of ineffective, self-defeating behaviors to avoid.

Goal

To assist trainees in better identifying what could obstruct or stop the communication process

Time Needed—Trainees' preparation: ¾ to 1¼ hours for the three exercises
Group work: ¾ to 1⅓ hours for the three exercises

Materials

- *Peer Power, Book One, Workbook* (one for each trainee)
- Flip chart paper or whiteboard
- Pencil or pen for each trainee
- Name tag for name on shirt
- Sticky notes for trainees to utilize during training
- Snacks for trainees if budget permits
- Crayons
- Koosh balls or other things to hold in their hands
- Rewards to give to trainees at appropriate times (M&M's, smiley faces, etc.)
- 3 × 5 notecards
- Optional: CD player and music to play to bring people back from break

Training Procedures

1. Teach the entire module in one session.
2. If you find that trainees need more practice on identification of communication stoppers and if your training schedule will permit, use a second session to continue the teaching techniques recommended.
3. For youth, ask them to take turns reading out loud the different communication stoppers.

Evaluation Process

You can determine the trainees' understanding by the responses you receive during the training session. The tendency may be for one or two trainees to take the initiative in answering, thus enabling some trainees to not become as involved as is desirable. Concern for the evaluation process will cause you to assure active participation by all trainees and increased involvement by individuals whose skills need improvement.

Measuring Outcomes

1. Degree of accuracy in discriminating communications stoppers can be determined by role-playing, Exercises 4.1 and 4.2, and other techniques used in the training session.

2. Degree of accuracy in identifying helpful responses can be determined by the responses provided to trainees' problems in one of the training techniques.

3. Can trainees recognize typical stoppers they use after this module and stop using some of the "stoppers"?

EXERCISE 4.1
RECOGNIZING COMMUNICATION STOPPERS

Goal

To help trainees learn the different kinds of communication exercises and be able to recognize them when used

Time Needed—Trainees' preparation: 30 to 45 minutes for this exercise
Group work: 45 to 60 minutes

Introduction to the Exercise

Memorizing the 11 kinds of communication stoppers is not the emphasis. Rather the emphasis is on increasing the trainees' recognition of the wide scope of activities frequently used that are ineffective in communication. The definitions, examples, and training session activities will enable the trainees to improve their communication behaviors.

The 11 communication stoppers are defined in the *Peer Power, Book One, Workbook*, Exercise 4.1, with sample statements provided for the trainees. You may want to ask the youth trainees to take turns reading each communication stopper. The 11 kinds, definitions of each, and examples (different from those provided in *Peer Power, Book One, Workbook*) are as follows:

1. **Directing, ordering**—to tell someone to do something in such a manner that gives the other person little or no choice. Example: "Get to work by 8:00 a.m."

2. **Warning, threatening**—to tell the other person that if the behavior continues, then certain consequences will happen. Example: "If you are not at work by 8:00 a.m., you may be docked."

3. **Moralizing, preaching**—to tell someone things he/she ought to do. Example: "You should help your coworker."

4. **Persuading, arguing**—to try to influence another person with facts, information, and logic. Example: "If you drop out of school, then you can't find a good job."

5. **Advising, recommending**—to provide answers for a problem. Example: "If I were you, I would quit being Jim's friend."

6. **Evaluating, criticizing**—to make a negative interpretation of another person's behavior. Example: "You got in to work so late, you must have been up to no good."

7. **Praising**—to make positive evaluations of another person's behavior. Example: "That is the most beautiful idea I have ever heard; you are great!"

8. **Supporting, sympathizing**—to try to talk the other person out of his/her feelings or to deny another person's feelings. Example: "Just wait, things will be better tomorrow. You will not feel as sad about losing your grandmother."

9. **Diagnosing**—to analyze the other person's behavior and communicate that you have their behaviors figured out. Example: "You must be depressed."

10. **Diverting, bypassing**—to change the subject or to not talk about the problem presented by the other person. Example: "I know you are having trouble with your friend, but all I want to know is, do you want to go to the movie?"

11. **Kidding, teasing**—to try to avoid talking about the problem by laughing or by distracting the other person. Example: "Why don't you just blow up your car since it doesn't work well?"

Training Procedures

1. Ask trainees to refer to Exercise 4.1 sheets as you explain and illustrate the 11 kinds of stoppers of communication. An option would be to have the trainees take turns reading each communication stopper.

2. Ask trainees to provide examples for each stopper as you teach it.

3. After discussing each stopper, model the behavior so as to enable the trainees to see, hear, and feel the effects.

4. Optional: Have trainees practice in dyads after each stopper is modeled so that each trainee experiences the use of the communication stopper in both the helper and helpee roles. This is where one trainee presents a problem, the partner responds with the stopper, and then the two reverse roles. Trainees are guided to discuss the feelings each person experienced after the stopper was communicated.

   Note: Eleven practice situations are to occur with each being done following the modeling of that specific communication stopper.

5. Distribute 3 × 5 index cards and ask each trainee to write one problem on a card. Tell trainees how the card will be used (Step 6).

6. Collect the cards after the problems have been written and select cards to which the trainees are to give responses.

   a. Read a card and ask each trainee to write a response on paper. The response is one that the trainee feels would be a helpful response to give as a helper.

   b. Reread the problem and have different trainees read responses as they wrote them.

   c. Ask trainees to identify the stoppers in the responses.

   d. Ask group members if they would continue talking about the problem if that response were given to them by a helper.

7. Optional Strategies

   a. Rate responses in terms of helpfulness.

(1) Have trainees write a problem on a 3 × 5 card and give it to the trainer. Then the trainer reads three problems. Trainees write their response to each problem and submit them to the trainer.

(2) The trainer reads the problem and several responses, asking the trainees to rate these responses in terms of helpfulness:

8. High (H) for when the response was very helpful. Medium (M) for when the response was helpful. Low (L) for when the response was not helpful.

   a. The trainer always rates the statement along with the trainees. Each person, including the trainer, is encouraged to explain his/her rating.

9. Collect Exercise 4.1 sheets.

10. Return Exercise 4.2 sheets with written comments.

Application for Trainees After the Group Meeting

1. Ask trainees to complete Exercises 4.2 and 4.3 and submit them at the next training session.

2. Ask trainees to come to the next session prepared to discuss Exercises 4.2 and 4.3.

EXERCISE 4.2
IDENTIFYING COMMUNICATION STOPPERS

Goal

To provide practice for trainees to identify different kinds of communication stoppers in comments

Time Needed—Trainees' preparation: 10 to 15 minutes for this exercise
Group work: 0 to 10 minutes

Introduction to the Exercise

Exercise 4.2 is designed to be done outside of the training session. Several statements are provided so that trainees can analyze the communication stoppers and identify the kind according to the list supplied in Exercise 4.1.

Training Procedures

1. Discuss with trainees the answers they recorded and why. The answers as we have them are as follows:

Answers	Stoppers
11	1. Kidding
10	2. Diverting
9	3. Diagnosing
8	4. Sympathizing
7	5. Praising
6	6. Criticizing
5	7. Advising
4	8. Persuading
3	9. Moralizing
2	10. Threatening
1	11. Ordering

2. Collect Exercise 4.2 sheets.

Application for Trainees After the Group Meeting

Assignments were made at close of Exercise 4.1.

EXERCISE 4.3
STOPPERS OK AT TIMES

Goal

To help trainees identify appropriate times to use communication stoppers

Time Needed—Trainees' preparation: 10 to 15 minutes for this
exercise
Group work: 0 to 10 minutes

Introduction to the Exercise

It is important that the trainees realize that at times one needs to use stoppers.

Training Procedures

1. Have trainees list times they would use stoppers.

2. List roles they might take on that are not helping roles.

Application for Trainees After the Group Meeting

1. Have trainees read the introduction to Module V.

2. Ask them to review and complete Exercise 5.1 before the next meeting.

3. Ask the trainees to complete the notes after Module V and ask one or two to share their reaction to Module V.

Unit B
DEVELOPING BASIC HELPING SKILLS

DEVELOPING BASIC HELPING SKILLS

Unit B will provide a step-by-step approach in teaching listening and responding skills. These skills are extremely important in teaching basic helping skills for peer helpers. These skills are sequential and need to be taught in such a manner that the trainee learns them well enough to utilize them.

Attending skill (Module V) is the first skill, which teaches the trainee how to utilize their body to attend to others. Module VI, on the empathy skill, will assist the trainee in learning how to listen for both content and feelings. Summarizing skill is presented in Module VII and will assist the trainee in putting all thoughts together and giving feedback to the helpee.

Module VIII, on questioning, will assist the trainee in learning open-ended questioning techniques to facilitate the communication. The helper is more effective if he/she can listen and respond in a genuine manner. Module IX will assist the trainee in learning how to be genuine. Module X will help the trainee learn assertiveness skills that respect others and still get the point across at home, school, and work. At times in working with others, the skill of confrontation (Module XI) is helpful in instigating change in others' behavior.

Finally, Module XII on problem solving will provide skills for the trainee to work with others individually or in groups to solve problems.

These skills provide the people skills and finally the task skills to help the training group move through problem areas and "storming" times so that they can become a fully functioning group.

MODULE **V**

ATTENDING SKILL

INTRODUCTION

Attending behavior relates most directly to the concept of helper respect for the helpee, which is demonstrated when undivided attention is given to the helpee.

Goals

To teach trainees the difference between effective and ineffective nonverbal attending skills

To teach trainees to be able to discriminate between effective and ineffective nonverbal attending behaviors

To teach trainees to communicate effective nonverbal attending behaviors

Time Needed—Trainees' preparation: 1½ to 1¾ hours for the six exercises
Group work: 2½ to 3½ hours for the six exercises

Materials

- *Peer Power, Book One, Workbook* (one for each trainee)
- Flip chart paper or whiteboard
- Pencil or pen for each trainee

- Name tag for name on shirt
- Sticky notes for trainees to utilize during training
- Snacks for trainees if budget permits
- Crayons
- Koosh balls or other things to hold in their hands
- Rewards to give to trainees at appropriate times (M&M's, smiley faces, etc.)
- Optional: CD player and music to play to bring people back from break
- Optional: Video equipment to be used to model skills taught or to tape the practice sessions of the trainees.

Training Procedures

Be prepared to do the demonstrations required to teach Module V as explained in Exercise 5.1, Training Procedures.

Evaluation Process

You can check on trainees' abilities to discriminate between effective and ineffective attending behaviors as they role-play and by reviewing the flow sheets.

Measuring Outcomes

1. The module goals are met when the trainees show high levels of attending behaviors. This can be subjectively measured by observing the attending behaviors of trainees when they function as helpers.
2. The lesson will be successful when all trainees are able to rate good attending behaviors accurately.

EXERCISE 5.1
EXAMPLES OF NONVERBAL
COMMUNICATION BEHAVIORS

Goal

To demonstrate effective and ineffective nonverbal attending skills

Time Needed—Trainees' preparation: 20 to 30 minutes for this exercise

Group work: 45 to 60 minutes

Introduction to the Exercise

Attending behavior is very important in peer helping and all positive interpersonal communications. Trainees are generally willing and eager to learn more about attending skills. Through video and/or demonstrations you will be able to increase their awareness of various attending skills and how the skills can be used more effectively.

The attending skills can be learned by young and old; however, because skills are ones with which they are not familiar, you will need to proceed step by step with sufficient examples and time for the trainees to incorporate their new experiences into their memory of previous experiences. Also, give them opportunities to participate and interact.

Training Procedures

1. Demonstrate (model) by video or practice (with trainer doing the modeling during the training session) nonverbal, nonattending behavior, such as not giving eye contact, nervous hand and body mannerisms, and not squaring the helper's body to face the helpee. Upon completion of the demonstration the trainees report their feelings generated by the nonattending behavior of the trainer or model in the video.

2. Have the trainees pair off and practice so as to experience nonverbal nonattending behavior as just modeled by the trainer. Trainees should change roles so that each has a chance to role-play both helpee and helper roles. Upon completion of the role-playing exercise, both partners report feelings generated by a helper's nonattending behavior.

3. Demonstrate on video or model minimal attending behaviors. Minimal attending behavior means giving the helpee eye contact and no other nonverbal cues of attending. Verbal behavior can be used without emphasis by noncommittal

words such as "um, yes." Upon completion of the demonstration, the trainees report their feelings generated by the minimal attending behavior of the trainer.

4. Have the trainees pair off and practice so as to experience the minimal attending behavior just modeled by the trainer. Trainees should change roles so that each has a chance to practice both helper and helpee. Upon completion of the practice exercise, both partners report feelings generated by a helper's minimal attending behavior.

5. Demonstrate on video or model attending behaviors. Attending behaviors include direct and consistent eye contact, leaning slightly forward in an open position, squaring the body to face the helpee, and showing through facial expression that the helper is listening attentively. Verbal behaviors can be used that are consistent with the concerns of the helpee but without emphasis.

6. Have trainees pair off and practice so as to experience the attending behavior just modeled by the trainer. Trainees should change roles so that each has a chance to role-play both helpee and helper. Upon completion of the role-playing exercise, both partners report feelings generated by a helper's attending behavior.

7. Use additional techniques for increasing the trainee's awareness of nonverbal communication, such as playing the camera game. Explain to the trainees that many a person's judgments about people are influenced by what he/she "sees" as opposed to really "knowing" the true picture. The camera game consists of the following:

   a. Each trainee selects a partner and faces that partner.

   b. Both partners close their eyes and think about their partner. Inform trainees that after a few seconds, they will open their eyes upon command and look directly at their partner to observe dress, hairstyle, posture, eyes, sex, age, and as many characteristics as they can observe about the partner.

   c. Have trainees close their eyes and think about what they saw and what conclusions can be drawn by what they saw. (For example, seeing a smile might lead a person to conclude that his/her partner was a happy person.)

d. Have trainees share with the group what they saw and the conclusions drawn from what they saw.

e. Have the trainees close their eyes and think about someone they know who reminds them of their partner.

f. Have the trainees share with their partners the type of person about whom they have been thinking.

8. Explain to the trainees that in the next training session (Exercise 5.2) they will be practicing the attending skills and providing each other with vital information on how they perform. Rating material (flow sheets) will be provided to help trainees provide feedback to each other.

9. Collect Exercise 5.1 sheets.

10. Return exercise sheets from Module IV, if not previously returned, with written comments and make any verbal comments at the same time that will help trainees' motivation and personal growth.

Application for Trainees After the Group Meeting

1. Ask each trainee to come prepared at the next training session to practice a concern (problem). Inform trainees that the role-playing is to be done in clusters of three and that the purpose is to provide experience for their partners to practice attending skills.

2. Ask trainees to read Exercise 5.2 and come prepared to use the exercise sheet during the training session.

EXERCISE 5.2
BECOMING AWARE OF MY ATTENDING
BEHAVIOR

Goal

To help trainees become aware of effective and ineffective nonverbal behavior

Time Needed—Trainees' preparation: no time needed for this
exercise

Group work: 30 to 45 minutes

Introduction to the Exercise

This exercise will help trainees gain a better understanding of how one feels with different attending behaviors being shown by another person.

Training Procedures

Follow the directions given in *Peer Power, Book One, Workbook*, Exercise 5.2.

Application for Trainees After the Group Meeting

1. Ask trainees to observe people's attending behaviors and the effects those behaviors have on other people.

2. Have them report their observations at the next training session.

EXERCISE 5.3
REACTIONS TO ATTENDING
AWARENESS ACTIVITY

Goal

To assist the trainee in an awareness of attending behavior

Time Needed—Trainees' preparation: 15 to 20 minutes for this
exercise

Group work: 15 to 20 minutes

Introduction to the Exercise

This exercise will give trainees experience in verbalizing the results of nonattending, minimal attending, and attending behavior.

Training Procedure

1. Have trainees fill out the infomation in the exercise.

2. It may be helpful to discuss this with the group.

Application for Trainees After the Group Meeting

1. Ask trainees to observe the nonverbal behavior of others.

2. Have them report their observations at the next training session.

EXERCISE 5.4
BECOMING AWARE OF OTHERS'
NONVERBAL BEHAVIOR

Goal

To help trainees tune into the nonverbal behavior of others

Time Needed—Trainees' preparation: 5 to 10 minutes for this exercise
Group work: 20 to 30 minutes

Introduction to the Exercise

This exercise can be a very moving experience. It is best to discuss the experience for a long period of time.

Training Procedures

1. Divide into pairs.

2. Follow directions in *Peer Power, Book One, Workbook*.

3. Discuss the experience at the completion.

Application for Trainees After the Group Meeting

Ask trainees to be observant of others after learning nonverbal signals.

EXERCISE 5.5
WORDS MEAN DIFFERENT THINGS
TO DIFFERENT PEOPLE

Goal

To help trainees focus on various slang words in their area and define what they mean

Time Needed—Trainees' preparation: 5 to 10 minutes for this exercise
Group work: 20 to 30 minutes

Introduction to the Exercise

This exercise will help trainees to begin thinking about some of the language used in their community. In order to be an effective listener they need to be aware of some of the various meanings of words.

Training Procedures

1. Ask trainees to write down unique words used by their family. Include definitions.

2. Ask trainees to share their words and definitions with others in the group.

3. Ask trainees to brainstorm words used by different cultural groups in their community.

4. Try to help trainees understand that words mean different things to different people and cultures.

Application for Trainees After the Group Meeting

1. Ask trainees to make a list of words in their local community that have different meanings than the standard dictionary definition.

2. Have them read Exercise 5.6 and be prepared to do it at the next meeting.

EXERCISE 5.6
RATING THE HELPER

Goal

To provide experiences for trainees to practice attending behaviors and learn how to evaluate the quality of the attending skills

Time Needed—Trainees' preparation: 10 to 20 minutes on this exercise
Group work: 20 to 30 minutes

Introduction to the Exercise

This entire training session is devoted to having trainees practice concerns so that attending skills can be practiced. These trainees will have an experience in feedback. Often they need assistance in providing feedback in a constructive manner that will be helpful to the receiver as well as to the person who does the rating.

Training Procedures

1. Collect application from Exercise 5.5.

2. Divide trainees into clusters of threes (triads). One person should assume the role of the helpee, one person the helper, and one the rater.

3. Have trainees refer to Exercise 5.6, "Rating the Helper," in *Peer Power, Book One, Workbook* and explain to trainees how the rating process operates.

4. Demonstrate the practice exercise, including helpee and helper activities, and the rater's job, including the marking of the flow sheet, and the feedback process. This procedure introduces the task of the rater. In order to explain the rater's task, the trainer will demonstrate by assuming the role of the helper. When the trainer in the role of helper responds to the helpee, the raters will evaluate the trainer's attending behavior according to the format in the

workbook, Exercise 5.6, second page, entitled "Attending Skill: Rating Flow Sheet."

5. Model with several responses and discuss afterward two or three responses how the rater would mark the flow sheet. Model until all trainees understand the rating process and the marking of the flow sheet.

6. Direct trainees to practice the skills of attending, rating, and providing feedback by repeating the model demonstrated by the trainer.

7. Discuss after the first role-playing in the clusters what occurred and how trainees felt. Supply additional information to facilitate the learning process.

8. Have trainees exchange roles so that each trainee has a chance to practice all three roles.

   Optional: Trainees can be filmed in groups of three as they practice their attending skills. Play these videos back to the large group with the audio turned off. Have the group rate the attending behavior of the helper.

9. Move from cluster to cluster to assist the trainees.

10. Discuss, as a group, what occurred and what they learned.

11. Return previously collected worksheets that have not yet been returned. Include written comments on the papers.

Application for Trainees After the Group Meeting

1. Have trainees practice attending this week.

2. Ask each trainee to identify by name someone he/she will attend to.

EXERCISE 5.7
SENSITIVITY TO ATTENDING TO
PEOPLE OF OTHER CULTURES

Goal

To help trainees identify how people from other cultures pay attention nonverbally

Time Needed—Trainees' preparation: 10 to 15 minutes for this exercise

Group work: 15 to 20 minutes

Trainees' preparation after the group meeting to complete the exercise: 20 to 30 minutes

Introduction to the Exercise

In a variety of cultures nonverbal behavior is very different. For example, in some Asian cultures, eye contact is not appropriate.

Training Procedures

1. Have the trainees identify other cultures in their community. Write those cultures on the chalkboard.

2. Ask them to identify appropriate attending behaviors of other cultures. For example: physical closeness, eye contact, touching. Put the attending behavior on the chalkboard.

3. Have the trainees discuss what kind of implications this has in terms of effective listening.

Application for Trainees After the Group Meeting

1. Ask trainees to write how different cultures will impact their attending skills.

2. Ask trainees to read the introduction to Module VI, *Peer Power, Book One, Workbook.*

3. Ask trainees to complete Exercise 6.1 before the next training session.

EMPATHY SKILL

INTRODUCTION

Module VI consists of several exercises and will require three or more training sessions. Empathy skill requires not only knowledge but also practice.

Empathic behavior is the skill of listening to others with understanding. The helper accurately perceives the meaning and feelings of the helpee. Generally, trainees would not have high ratings in empathic behaviors prior to the training sessions; therefore, Module VI takes on new emphasis because empathy is so important in peer helping.

Goals

To enable trainees to learn and use empathy—accurately perceiving the meaning and feelings of the helpee and then communicating the understanding to the helpee

To enable trainees to summarize what the helpee has been saying in such a manner that it will give new light and insight to the helpee

Time Needed—Trainees' preparation: 2¼ to 3½ hours for the nine exercises
Group work: 4¼ to 6½ hours for the nine exercises

Materials

- *Peer Power, Book One, Workbook* (one for each trainee)
- Flip chart paper or whiteboard
- Pencil or pen for each trainee
- Name tag for name on shirt
- Sticky notes for trainees to utilize during training
- Snacks for trainees if budget permits
- Crayons
- Koosh balls or other things to hold in their hands
- Rewards to give to trainees at appropriate times (M&M's, smiley faces, etc.)
- Optional: CD player and music to play to bring people back from break
- Optional: Video equipment to be used to model skills taught or to tape the practice sessions of the trainees
- Teaching tool: *Feelings: The 3 Rs—Receiving, Reflecting, Responding* (Tindall & Salmon, 1993)

Training Procedures

1. Review training time, length of each session, and ability of trainees to learn new material. Depending on the trainees' skill level, you may want to shorten or combine some of the exercises. For example, if the trainees have already learned skills in previous peer programs, they may already have good empathy skills.

2. Devise an approach to Module VI so as to divide the nine exercises into convenient groupings—for example, introduction to Module VI and Exercise 6.1 covered in one session, Exercises 6.2 and 6.3 in another, or consider whether the procedure should be slower (then do only 6.2) or faster (then perhaps do 6.2, 6.3, 6.4) in one session. The time suggested for each exercise and your time block per session may be combined to aid you in how you can group exercises.

3. Remember persons with Feeling types of personality will have a hard time with Exercise 6.1. Thinking types will have a hard time with Exercise 6.3.

4. If trainees are having difficulty learning empathy, to supplement the material you may want to use the book *Feelings: The 3 Rs—Receiving, Reflection, Responding* (Tindall & Salmon, 1993).

Measuring Outcomes

1. Identify the degree of accuracy in discriminating the effectiveness of helpers' responses in all exercises within the module.

2. Identify the degree of accuracy in helpers' responses to feeling and meaning in all exercises within the module.

3. Determine the accuracy in responses to exercises that identify discrimination and communication of empathy.

EXERCISE 6.1
DISCRIMINATING AND RESPONDING
BY PARAPHRASING

Goal

To enable trainees to discriminate and respond by paraphrasing the helpee's concerns without changing the meanings of those concerns as expressed and felt by the helpee

Time Needed—Trainees' preparation: 30 to 45 minutes for this exercise
Group work: 30 to 60 minutes

Introduction to the Exercise

Paraphrasing will need to be explained as well as the purposes for using paraphrasing. The use of paraphrasing can be taught best by modeling and having trainees practice the skill. Use of films, filmstrips, prepared videos, and/or trainer modeling is an effective means of introducing the paraphrasing.

Trainees may be concerned only about words used by the helpee. Stress the importance of understanding the feeling expressed and the intended message as well as the words in order to paraphrase accurately the concerns as expressed and felt by the helpee. This will take time to learn and will require repeated experience with meaningful feedback.

Training Procedures

1. Discuss what is meant by a paraphrase and give examples such as:

   Example: "My parents don't let me go anywhere I enjoy going."

   Paraphrase: "Your parents don't let you go places you like to go."

2. Refer trainees to Exercise 6.1, and have them write a helper response for the first helpee statement.

3. Have trainees share their response individually and discuss the response with constructive feedback.

4. Have trainees repeat this procedure for the second helpee statement. As responses are shared, have the trainees rate each response according to the rating scale for paraphrasing, provided in Exercise 6.1, *Peer Power, Book One, Workbook.*

5. Show previously prepared video of low, medium, and high paraphrasing (if no video equipment is available this procedure may be omitted).

6. Model paraphrasing behavior by the trainer being a helper to a trainee who presents a problem. The group individually rates the trainer's response as high, medium, or low according to the rating scale for paraphrasing.

7. By moving around the total group circle, have each person serve as a helper to the person next to him/her while the other trainees in the group rate the helper's response. Have the trainees explain their ratings. The trainer should rate last.

Note: In teaching paraphrasing, the trainer would be wise to explain the need for the helper to repeat silently the exact words in order to assure self-understanding before putting the response into an accurate paraphrase comment.

8. Continue moving around the circle until the trainees are fairly consistent in their ratings with other trainees.

9. Ask trainees to form clusters of three, and follow the directions provided in Exercise 6.1, to complete the exercise (as trainer, move from group to group and assist where needed).

10. Collect application for Exercises 5.7.

11. Return previously collected Exercise 5.4 sheets with written comments.

Application for Trainees After the Group Meeting

Ask trainees to read and complete Exercise 6.2 before the next group meeting.

EXERCISE 6.2
FEELING WORDS

Goal

To enable trainees to learn additional feeling words and to increase their awareness of feeling words

Time Needed—Trainees' preparation: 20 to 30 minutes for this exercise
Group work: 30 to 45 minutes

Introduction to the Exercise

In Exercise 6.1, the trainees improved their paraphrasing and may have started to understand their feelings. Often individuals are unable to think of feeling words, and unless they have the vocabulary, it will be difficult to learn the feeling part of empathy. This exercise will at least give them a vocabulary.

Training Procedures

1. Ask the trainees to read the list of feeling words.

2. Using the whole group, brainstorm additional words. Have the trainees write them.

3. Have the trainees look at the exercises and respond by using feeling words from the list.

4. Ask each person to give a statement, to which the person next to him/her responds using one of the feeling words.

   Note: A resource book with 48 "feeling faces" that may be used to help trainees learn vocabulary and relate facial expressions with feelings is Feelings: The 3 Rs—Receiving, Reflecting, Responding *by J. Tindall and S. Salmon, 1993, Accelerated Development Inc.*

Application for Trainees After the Group Meeting

1. Go over the assignment according to the exercises that have been planned to be covered in the next training session.

2. Have trainees complete Exercises 6.3 and 6.4 or whatever exercises are planned to be covered in the next training session.

EXERCISE 6.3
RESPONDING TO FEELINGS

Goal

To enable trainees to understand and respond to helpee's feelings

Time Needed—Trainees' preparation: 15 to 30 minutes for this exercise
Group work: 30 to 45 minutes

Introduction to the Exercise

In Exercises 6.1 and 6.2, the trainees improved their paraphrasing, and may have started to understand and include in their responses an understanding of the helpee's feelings.

During Exercise 6.3 the emphases are upon understanding and responding to those feelings. The trainee needs to hear all of the meaning expressed by the helpee. Even though stress may be upon words expressed by the helpee, also assist the trainees in being aware of understanding feelings by how the words are expressed, for example, tone differences, quality variances, rate of speech, and body movements.

Training Procedures

1. Discuss what is meant by feelings.

   Optional: Distribute a list of feeling words so that trainees can better understand what is meant by feelings.

2. Discuss the importance of not only listening for words but also listening for feelings.

3. Teach the helper to respond to a helpee's statement in the following manner.

"You feel _____
_____
_____ **because** _____
_____
_____.**"**

   This response paraphrases accurately the feelings and the meaning of the helpee's statement.

   Example—Helpee: "This has been a very rough week."

   Helper: "You feel (tired, exhausted, worn out) because it's been a very rough week."

4. Model the behavior being taught. Trainees then rate the trainer's responses based upon accuracy of feeling and meaning communicated.

   Optional: Show previously prepared video of behaviors to be taught.

5. Have trainees share responses to helpee's statements in Exercise 6.3. As one trainee shows a response; have others discuss the feeling expressed by the response; for example, teach them how to provide meaningful feedback to the trainee (helper) who shared the response.

6. After the trainer has modeled the behavior, have two train-ees practice in front of the total group with one trainee given the task of being a helper to another trainee (helpee). The helpee is to make one statement, the helper one response, and then the response is rated by the group. The rest of the group rates high (H), medium (M), and low (L), and gives feedback to the helper. Each trainee is required to give a rating of high (H), medium (M), or low (L) to the helper's responses according to the rating in Exercise 6.6, *Peer Power, Book One, Workbook.*

7. As trainees develop the facility for discriminating feelings, provide them with alternative response patterns such as:

"You sound..."

"You're angry because..."

"It bothers you that..."

8. Have trainees identify other alternative response patterns.

9. Emphasize that the helper's communication should accu-rately reflect the position of the helpee relative to his/her immediate feelings and the reason or conditions that are generating those feelings. Example of being accurately aware of the helpee's position:

Helpee's thought: "I see the dog."

Helpee's statement: "Will the dog bite?"

Helper's thought: "She is afraid of the dog."

Helper's statement: "You're afraid the dog will bite you."

10. Optional: Have trainees practice in triads with one member taking the role of helpee and making a statement, another member being helper and paraphrasing the statement to respond to meaning and feeling, and third member pro-viding feedback after the response (this may be postponed until Exercise 6.4 is taught).

Application for Trainees After the Group Meeting

1. If time elapses between Exercises 6.3 and 6.4, ask train-ees to record five statements they hear made by others in

which feelings are expressed. Following each statement, the trainee is to write the response he/she as helper would make to that statement and be prepared to discuss with the other trainees. Have trainees submit the material to you at the next training session.

2. Assign Exercise 6.4 in *Peer Power, Book One, Workbook* that are to be covered at next session.

EXERCISE 6.4
FEELINGS AND EMOTIONS

Goal

To enable trainees to examine how different words may be used to express similar meanings and how the "strength" of a word can communicate different feelings and emotions

Time Needed—Trainees' preparation: 15 to 30 minutes for this exercise
Group work: 30 to 45 minutes

Introduction to the Exercise

Exercise 6.4 is an extension of Exercise 6.3. The trainees need to review words that express feelings and emotions and to examine how different words with similar meaning can communicate different feelings and emotions. The exercise contains examples of words and the trainees will be able to brainstorm many more so as to expose them to a pool of words for their use in paraphrasing meanings expressed by the helpee.

Training Procedures

1. Discuss the purpose of Exercise 6.4 and the importance for the trainees.

2. Review with trainees their responses to Exercise 6.4 sheets and their reasons for different responses given.

3. Have trainees brainstorm feeling words and distinguish between feeling words that show different levels of emotion.

Example: gentle—strong—very strong—annoyed—irritated — "ticked off."

4. Have trainees practice in triads the concepts being taught. Have trainees take roles so that one is helper, one is helpee, and one is providing feedback (rater). Have them change roles and do the role-play three times so that each of the roles is performed by each trainee.

5. Collect Exercises 6.3 and 6.4 sheets.

6. Return Exercises 5.7 and 6.1 sheets with written comments.

Application for Trainees After the Group Meeting

Assign the exercises in *Peer Power, Book One, Workbook* that are to be covered at the next session (will need to have at least Exercise 6.5 completed).

EXERCISE 6.5
DESCRIBING FEELINGS

Goal

To increase trainees' ability to respond to the hidden and surface feelings of the helpee

Time Needed—Trainees' preparation: 15 to 20 minutes for this exercise
Group work: 30 to 45 minutes

Introduction to the Exercise

Feelings may be obvious (surface feelings), may not be expressed, or may be withheld intentionally. The underlying or hidden feelings are very important in peer helping. Exercise 6.5 is done to help trainees focus on both hidden and surface feelings. To be effective, a helper must respond accurately to hidden feelings. Prepare a list of feeling words and distribute to trainees.

Training Procedures

1. Discuss hidden and surface feelings and help trainees understand why they exist, the importance of the helper responding to both, and how the helper may recognize hidden feelings.

2. Discuss the responses trainees have for the situations in Exercise 6.5. Have one trainee give a response and others identify words used to respond to the different kinds of feelings.

3. Use a technique to demonstrate hidden and surface feelings and involve the trainees in the responses.

   a. Example: Boy about to fight.

   The trainer plays the role of a boy about to fight another boy. The activity works best when the trainer goes around the room in progression, having each group member respond to one of the trainer's feelings.

   If a trainee makes an accurate response, proceed to the next person, express another feeling, and wait for a response. When a trainee gives an inaccurate response or uses another category, coach the trainee to improve. Do not hold standards that are too high at this early stage of developing listening skills.

   This exercise is excellent to demonstrate difficulty in developing empathic responses and is an opportunity to point out some pitfalls and errors.

   b. Example: Boy angry with another boy.

   The trainer plays the role of a boy who is angry with another boy in a math class and has determined to do something about his anger.

   The following statements of feelings the trainer will use in the dialogue are to be used in sequence:

   "There is this kid in my math class who really bugs me."

   "He always picks on me and calls me names."

   "I think I'm going to punch him in the nose the next time he calls me a name."

From this point forward, the trainer responds flexibly to the helpee's response and develops discussion of the problem along these lines:

"Concerned about what might happen to me."

"Concerned about what the teacher will do."

"Concerned about what the principal will do."

"Concerned about what parents will do."

"Concerned about what other boy will do."

"Maybe the boy is just trying to bug me."

"Maybe I can ignore him."

c. Example: Worker creating a fight with coworker (notes to trainer—follow same instructions as for boy about to fight).

The trainer role-plays an assembly line worker about to fight another assembly line worker.

"There is this guy on the line that really bugs me."

"He is always calling me names and smarts off to me."

"I think I am going to punch him in the nose the next time he calls me a name."

From this point, the trainer responds flexibly to the helpee's response and develops the problem along these lines:

"Concerned about what might happen because he is much bigger."

"Concerned that I might get fired."

"Concerned about what will happen to my family."

"Concerned about whether I could get another job because I do not have a high school diploma."

"Maybe he has some hang-up."

"Maybe I can ignore him."

4. Collect Exercise 6.5 sheets.

5. Return Exercises 6.3 and 6.4 sheets with written comments.

Application for Trainees After the Group Meeting

1. Assign the exercises in *Peer Power, Book One, Workbook* that are to be covered at the next session (Exercise 6.6 needs to be studied but no written work needs to be prepared).

2. Ask trainees to study the exercises and come prepared to do and/or discuss them at the next session.

EXERCISE 6.6
PARAPHRASING FEELING: RATING THE HELPER

Goal

To improve trainees' ability to determine the effectiveness of paraphrasing feelings

Time Needed—Trainees' preparation: 10 to 15 minutes for this exercise
Group work: 30 to 45 minutes

Introduction to the Exercise

In the previous exercises trainees had to practice and provide feedback to each other. By now they should be ready to focus attention on how well they can determine whether or not a helper's response is effective in paraphrasing feelings and emotions.

Assist the trainees in focusing their feedback on the behavior instead of the person (helper). Have them provide feedback on what was done rather than what the helper was trying to do. If the person who provides the feedback is able to suggest another way and why, then have those suggestions made but only after giving feedback on what actually was done. The focus is not what was observed (i.e., helper behaviors seen and heard) by the rater but inferences (i.e., interpretations and conclusions) made by the rater, even though the inferences are based on what was observed.

Training Procedures

1. Point out the importance of the rater and what can be learned by doing the rating and by being rated.

2. Listen to and respond to feelings and concerns expressed by the trainees about rating.

3. Model two helper responses before rating (suggested that trainer take the role of helper during the modeling). To rate more accurately the level of helper responses, a series of two or more helper responses is often needed, thus enabling the rater to hear and see the helpee statement and other behavior following the helper's first response. In modeling the responses use two helper responses and then rate. The pattern is as follows:

Helpee: Statement of concern made.

Helper: Paraphrased response to show helpee that helper understands the concern and the feelings and emotions associated with the concern.

Helpee: Follow-through statement that often is a further self-exploration, a repeat of the first statement, or a less revealing statement than the first one.

Helper: Additional paraphrasing.

Rater: Provides feedback on observations (seen and heard) of helper's behaviors in responding to concerns, including feelings and emotions.

Example: Helpee: "This has been a very rough week."

Helper: "You feel (tired, exhausted, worried) because it has been a rough week."

Helpee: "Yes, but the weekend is coming up, and I'm excited."

Helper: "Even though the week has been rough, you feel excited about the weekend."

4. Have the trainees rate the trainer during the modeling.

5. Repeat the modeling until the ratings by the trainees are almost all the same for each practice round.

6. Ask the trainees to form triads and follow the directions for completing Exercise 6.6, Part A.

7. Move from cluster (triad) to cluster, assisting where needed.

8. After each practice round in the triads, have trainees discuss as a total group the concerns and feelings they have.

9. After completing three practice rounds in the triad (i.e., each trainee has practiced helpee, helper, and rater), introduce three helper responses in which the pattern is helpee, helper, helpee, helper, helpee, helper, and the feedback by rater. The purpose is to work toward the helper being able to use what is being learned not only to respond to each helpee statement but also to make a series of responses that will lead to complete peer helping sessions. Model the three response patterns.

10. Have trainees continue as directed by the workbook and complete Exercise 6.6, Part B.

11. Collect Exercise 6.6 sheets.

12. Return Exercise 6.5 sheets with written comments.

Application for Trainees After the Group Meeting

1. Assign the exercises in *Peer Power, Book One, Workbook* that are to be covered at the next session (Exercise 6.7 needs to be studied but no written work needs to be prepared).

2. Ask trainees to study Exercise 6.7 and come prepared to do it at the next session.

EXERCISE 6.7
RATING THE HELPER ON ATTENDING
AND EMPATHY

Goal

To give trainees experience in practicing skills of both attending and empathy

Time Needed—Trainees' preparation: 10 to 15 minutes for this exercise
Group work: 30 to 45 minutes

Introduction to the Exercise

The trainees have practiced attending skill (Module V) and empathy skill (Module VI) and should be ready to combine the skills in responding to situations. The Peer Helper Training Program is designed to teach a skill and then combine that skill with previously learned skills.

The teaching technique utilized is trainees interacting with each other through playing a role, talking about a concern, and rating one another. The Rating Flow Sheet is provided to facilitate recording feeling words and ratings of the helper's response in terms of feelings, paraphrased meanings, and attending. This is known as interactive teaching.

Training Procedures

1. Explain the purpose and procedure for Exercise 6.7.

2. Respond to and have trainees discuss concerns they have as a result of reviewing Exercise 6.7.

3. Remind trainees that the Rating Scale for Attending Behavior is in Exercise 5.6 and the Rating Scale for Empathy Response is in Exercise 6.7.

4. Review the job of the rater who is to rate each response made by the helpee: (1) Feeling word, (2) Quality of feeling word (how accurate), (3) Accuracy of responding to helpee's meaning, and (4) Level of attending. (Refer to Rating Flow Sheet in Exercise 6.7 in *Peer Power, Book One, Workbook.*) An example of words and their respective ratings for the Rating Flow Sheet would be as follows:

Feeling words	Feeling	Meaning	Attending
1. Concerned	H M L	H M L	H M L
2. Worried	H M L	H M L	H M L
3. Upset	H M L	H M L	H M L
4. No feeling word	H M L	H M L	H M L

5. Ask the rater to rate all three responses before feedback is given to the helpee.

6. Encourage the helpee to use the same problems in sequential practice interchanges. This process develops depth, consistency, and direction toward problem solving and cuts down the necessity of presenting a new problem each time. Guide trainees to use the same concern for each of their four initiating statements.

7. Demonstrate the process by taking the role of helper and having the total group rate the trainer and discuss their ratings after each role-play.

   Optional:

   a. Show video example of high, medium, and low responses.

   b. The trainer may use a video and replay it for the group.

   c. The trainer may provide helpers with example of problems if trainees have none of their own.

8. Ask the trainees to cluster in triads and follow directions for completing Exercise 6.7.

9. Move from cluster to cluster and provide assistance where needed.

10. Stop the role-playing periodically and have trainees share and discuss their experiences.

11. Collect Exercise 6.7 sheets.

12. Return Exercise 6.6 sheets with your written comments.

Application for Trainees After the Group Meeting

1. Assign the exercises in *Peer Power, Book One, Workbook* that are to be covered at the next session (Exercise 6.8 needs to be studied and the application completed prior to the next session; directions are within the exercise).

2. Ask trainees to come prepared to discuss Exercise 6.8.

EXERCISE 6.8
FACILITATIVE AND NONFACILITATIVE DIALOGUE

Goal

To enable trainees to grasp the extended dialogue between helpee and helper and to recognize differences between a facilitative and a nonfacilitative helper

Time Needed—Trainees' preparation: 30 to 45 minutes for this exercise
Group work: 10 to 15 minutes

Introduction to the Exercise

Exercise 6.8 is designed so that it can be used during a training session or totally as an application activity. Through studying the two dialogues, trainees will be able to understand how the helper can assist the helpee to probe into an expressed concern.

The directions for analysis of Dialogues I and II are for trainees to identify communication stoppers that occur in Dialogue II. Trainees then are directed to explain how the two differ, which hopefully will cause trainees to analyze their own behaviors and consider how to improve their own helper behaviors.

Training Procedures

1. Have trainees complete Exercise 6.8 prior to training session.

2. Dramatize the two dialogues by having trainees read the dialogue.

3. Discuss the two dialogues and the response labels that the trainees chose for each helper response. The responses as we key them are as follows:

Dialogue I			Dialogue II		
Item number	Response letter	Kind of response	Item number	Response letter	Kind of response
6	A	Advising	39	O	Open-ended questions
8	A	Advising	41	M	Empathic responding (H)
10	G	Moralizing	43	R	Underlying feelings
12	H	Persuading	45	R	Underlying feelings
14	D	Diverting	47	M	Empathic responding (H)
16	G	Preaching	49	M	Empathic responding (H)
18	P	Paraphrase words	51	R	Underlying feelings
20	N	Minimal responding	53	M	Empathic responding (H)
22	F	Kidding	55	M	Empathic responding (H)
24	D	Diverting	57	R	Underlying feelings
26	H	Preaching	59	M	Empathic responding (H)
28	N	Minimal responding	61	M	Empathic responding (H)
30	H	Persuading	63	M	Empathic responding (H)
32	J	Supporting	65	M	Empathic responding (H)
34	D	Diverting	67	M	Empathic responding (H)
			69	M	Empathic responding (H)
			71	R	Underlying feelings
			73	O	Open-ended questions
			75	M	Empathic responding (H)
			77	J	Supporting
			79	O	Open-ended questions

Application for Trainees After the Group Meeting

1. Assign exercises in *Peer Power, Book One, Workbook* that are to be covered at the next session (Exercise 6.9 is to be completed before the next training session).

2. Ask trainees to review Exercise 6.9 and come prepared to do and/or discuss them at the next training session.

3. Hear and respond to trainees' concerns pertaining to Empathy Skill, Module VI.

4. Collect Exercise 6.8 sheets.

5. Return Exercise 6.7 sheets (and Exercise 6.6 sheets if not previously done) with written comments.

EXERCISE 6.9
CHOOSE THE BEST EMPATHY RESPONSE

Goal

To provide the trainees with experience in choosing the best response from among three possible responses for each situation

Time Needed—Trainees' preparation: 10 to 15 minutes for this exercise
Group work: 15 to 30 minutes

Introduction to the Exercise

The exercise will enable you to examine how well trainees can select the best response among possible ones. The exercise requires a minimal amount of time to complete the selection, but discussion among trainees can be extensive and interesting.

Training Procedures

1. Discuss with trainees the outcomes desired from them doing the exercise.

2. Discuss the responses they have for the three situations and include in the discussion the three questions raised in Direction #4. The best response for each situation as we have keyed it is as follows:

Situation A: Response 2

Situation B: Response 1

Situation C: Response 1

Situation D: Response 1

3. Discuss trainees' comments from their application for Analysis of Dialogues I and II, last page of Exercise 6.8.

4. Collect Exercise 6.8 sheets.

5. Return Exercise 6.7 sheets with your written comments if not done previously.

Application for Trainees After the Group Meeting

1. Have trainees complete Exercise 6.9 outside of training session.

   Optional: Assign trainees in clusters of two or three to do Exercise 6.9 together outside of training sessions. The purpose is to enable them to discuss and share the various points with each other.

2. Collect Exercise 6.9 sheets at next training session.

3. Return Exercise 6.7 sheets during the next training session with written comments if not done previously.

4. Ask them to complete the notes at the end of the module on empathy. Have a discussion with the total group concerning their reaction to the empathy skill.

5. Read the introduction to Module VII.

MODULE **VII**

SUMMARIZING SKILL

INTRODUCTION

Developing summarizing responses is a skill that involves listening completely to the helpee's concerns and then summarizing the problem in the helpee's own words while adding to the summary new insight into the helpee's problem. The helper attempts to shed new light and adds additional dimensions of awareness to the problem by using initiative responses.

The helper must be very attentive to the helpee. In Module VI trainees practiced and developed their attending and empathy skills. The trainees, who are participating well in the training program and who demonstrate promise of being effective peer helpers, are able, at this stage of their development, to capture important thoughts and feelings expressed in the extended interchange. They need now to be able to feed back to the helpee the most important parts plus enable the helpee to gain new insights. Summarizing skill will enable the trainee to do so.

Goals

To enable trainees to learn summarizing skill, which involves listening to helper's concerns

To learn to summarize not only with helpee's words but also adding words in such a manner that the helpee will gain new insights and added dimensions of awareness about the problem

Materials

- *Peer Power, Book One, Workbook* (one for each trainee)
- Flip chart paper or whiteboard
- Pencil or pen for each trainee
- Name tag for name on shirt
- Sticky notes for trainees to utilize during training
- Snacks for trainees if budget permits
- Crayons
- Koosh balls or other things to hold in their hands
- Rewards to give to trainees at appropriate times (M&M's, etc.)

Time Needed—Trainees' preparation: 1 to 1½ hours for two exercises
Group work: ¾ to 1¾ hours for two exercises with group work optional for Exercise 7.2

Training Procedures

1. Review training session time to determine whether Exercise 7.2 is to be done as an application only or as an application plus a training session.
2. Review the total Module VII before starting to teach it.
3. Prepare for the demonstrations and/or the video equipment use.

Evaluation Process

The effectiveness of the training process can be determined by the trainees' interaction in the techniques being employed. Their involvement, level of participation, and concerns expressed can help determine what is occurring within them.

Measuring Outcomes

1. Measure summarizing responses by trainees' responses during demonstrations and during their practice in triads.

2. Measure effectiveness in understanding and analyzing summarizing responses by flow sheets in Exercise 7.1.

3. Measure application of skills by Exercise 7.2 sheets.

EXERCISE 7.1
SUMMARIZING: RATING THE HELPER'S RESPONSES

Goal

To enable trainees to study examples of, to practice making, and to evaluate summarizing responses

Time Needed—Trainees' preparation: 10 to 15 minutes for this exercise
Group work: 45 to 60 minutes

Introduction to the Exercise

Exercise 7.1 in *Peer Power, Book One, Workbook* provides an example of an extended dialogue that contains summarizing responses. By having the trainees review the dialogue they will be able to understand better the extended dialogue process and how the summarizing responses can assist peer helping.

In addition to the dialogue, the trainees will probably benefit from demonstrations with discussions. Following each demonstration, have other trainees rate helpers. Then discuss the rating made by each and the bases for the rating, thus enabling trainees to observe an extended dialogue and response summarization, make a rating, and discuss the dialogue and rating.

Exercise 7.1 is designed to involve trainees and to provide modeling and feedback so that each trainee will develop the summarizing skill. The training session may be entered by some trainees with anxiety; however, the anxiety can be overcome through modeling and sufficient practice in the total group before asking them to role-play in triads.

Training Procedures

1. Discuss summarizing skill, its use, and its purposes.

2. Review examples of a lead for a helper's summary response. Examples would include the following:

    a. "What I hear you really saying is..."

    b. "It seems to me what you're saying is..."

    c. "The real meaning behind what you're saying is..."

    d. "The real meaning behind what you're feeling is..."

    e. "The important points seem to be..."

3. Review the extended dialogue in *Peer Power, Book One, Workbook*, Exercise 7.1, and assist trainees with concerns they have relating to the dialogue.

    a. Assist trainees in listing the points expressed by the helpee.

       (1) Helpee is angry at a teacher for saying and doing two different things.

       (2) Helpee's boss makes a promise and then changes his/her mind.

       (3) Even the helpee's mom pushes him/her.

       (4) The helpee is fed up with school.

    b. Help trainees learn about initiative responses that can and should be used at times when summarizing with helpee's words could be used. The initiative response is a means of assisting the helpee in gaining increased awareness of the problem and insight into alternatives. An example of an initiative response that could be used in place of helper response Number 14 in the extended dialogue example would be the following:

"What I hear you saying is that you don't like being controlled, and you feel angry because you have no control over yourself. You would like to say to everyone that you can do what you want to do, and you will by quitting school."

4. Discuss the Rating Scale for Summarizing Responses provided in *Peer Power, Book One, Workbook*, Exercise 7.1.

5. Demonstrate an extended dialogue with a summarizing response and have each trainee rate the summarizing response. Discuss the ratings and the bases for them.

6. Model an extended dialogue, but just before making the summarizing response, stop the modeling and have the trainees identify the major points listed by the helpee (make a list on the chalkboard or flip pad). Then have trainees each write a summarizing response that they would give. Share and discuss the written responses. Have trainees provide feedback to the helper (trainee who has just shared a written summarizing response).

   Optional: By means of video, play an extended dialogue and stop the video just prior to summarizing response. Have trainees write a summarizing response, and then play the video response.

7. Cluster trainees in triads and have them follow the directions in Exercise 7.1. Move from cluster to cluster and assist where needed.

   Optional: Video one or more clusters during the practice and then play the video for their review and comments.

8. After trainees have completed the first extended dialogue, have them share their feelings and concerns.

9. Continue the activities in the triads until each trainee has been in each role—helpee, helper, and rater.

10. Collect sheets from Exercises 6.9 and 7.1.

Application for Trainees After the Group Meeting

Ask trainees to complete Exercise 7.2 before the next training session.

EXERCISE 7.2
USING YOUR NEW SKILLS: YOUR DIARY

Goal

To have trainees practice their new skills with persons they know other than members of the training program and to have trainees analyze what and how they did

Time Needed—Trainees' preparation: 20 to 30 minutes
Group work: 30 to 45 minutes if group
meeting is held (optional)

Introduction to the Exercise

The trainees have learned and practiced three basic communication skills—attending, empathy, and summarizing. Trainees took the Peer Helping Training Program with the intent of helping others. Now is a good time for trainees to practice their skills with other people.

This exercise is designed to have trainees use their learned skills as they associate with others in everyday life. As they use the skills, trainees are directed to keep a diary in which they analyze what and how they did. Therefore, this exercise is primarily to be completed as an application, and if training session time is spent, the time would be spent on sharing what was done, discussing the experiences and feelings trainees have, and assisting them in improving their skills.

Training Procedures

1. Review during the time of the assignment of Exercise 7.2 the purpose of the exercise and the exercise sheets where the information is to be recorded.

2. Make the exercise primarily an application.

3. If training session time is spent, use the time in having trainees share their experiences, feelings, and written comments. Have trainees assist one another in improving their skills.

4. Collect Exercise 7.2 sheets.

5. If a training session is held, return sheets from Exercise 6.9 and 7.1 with written comments.

Application for Trainees After the Group Meeting

1. If no training session time is spent on Exercise 7.2, then the application is assigned following Exercise 7.1.

2. If training session time is spent on Exercise 7.2, then ask trainees to complete Exercise 8.1 and review Exercise 8.2 before the next training session.

3. Ask the trainees to complete the NOTES to Module VII: Summarizing Skill and share their comments. How does the summarizing skill relate to their daily lives?

MODULE **VIII**

QUESTIONING SKILL

INTRODUCTION

Questioning is an important part of the dialogue between helpee and helper. Questioning in a skillful manner so as to be helpful to the helpee requires understanding and practice by the helper.

Module VIII is designed to provide information about questioning skill, the differences between open-ended questions and closed questions, and purposes for which questions can be helpful in the dialogue. The trainees are asked to prepare material (questions) on their own and obtain feedback by role-playing the behaviors during the training session, obtaining rater feedback, and practicing the skill with friends and recording what occurs. The trainer can make these experiences very meaningful for trainees.

Generally one or two training sessions are needed, plus time to prepare material between sessions. If trainees are quick learners and training sessions are approximately 60 minutes or more, then Exercises 8.1 and 8.2 can be done in one session: otherwise, do one in each of two sessions. Exercise 8.3 is to be done as an application with training time depending on what you feel is needed to facilitate trainees' development.

Goal

To enable the trainees to improve their questioning skill

Time Needed—Trainees' preparation: 1½ to 2⅓ hours for four exercises
Group work: 1 to 2¼ hours for four exercises

Materials

- *Peer Power, Book One, Workbook* (one for each trainee)
- Flip chart paper or whiteboard
- Pencil or pen for each trainee
- Name tag for name on shirt
- Sticky notes for trainees to utilize during training
- Snacks for trainees if budget permits
- Crayons
- Koosh balls or other things to hold in their hands
- Rewards to give to trainees at appropriate times (M&M's, etc.)
- Optional: Video equipment with previously produced video containing one or more examples of the behavior being taught
- Optional: CD to play music to bring trainees together (you may want to have a theme song or music by this time such as "Lean on Me" or other appropriate music agreed upon by the group)

Training Procedures

1. Review the total Module VIII to understand the scope.
2. Plan to cover the material in one or two sessions, depending upon available time for each session and how well the trainees are able to comprehend new material.
3. Proceed as suggested in the specific training procedures for each of the exercises.

Evaluation Process

A determination can be made of how well trainees are learning by analyzing the feedback obtained during the training sessions and from the exercise sheets they prepare. If trainees are having difficulty, one may need to use one or more training sessions for review and additional practice before progressing into additional material in *Peer Power, Book One, Workbook.*

Measuring Outcomes

1. Measure trainees' ability to know the difference between open-ended and closed questions by the application preparation done for Exercise 8.1.

2. Measure recognition and effectiveness of use by what occurs during practice rounds, recording, and feedback in Exercise 8.2.

3. Measure application by what occurs when questioning skill is used with friends in completing Exercise 8.3.

EXERCISE 8.1
OPEN INVITATIONS TO TALK
(OPEN-ENDED QUESTIONS)

Goal

To enable trainees to learn how to use questioning effectively and to keep the interchange going with the helpee

Time Needed—Trainees' preparation: 45 to 60 minutes for this exercise
Group work: 30 to 45 minutes

Introduction to the Exercise

The open-ended question encourages the helpee to explore oneself and concerns held. Through use of open-ended questions, the helper also communicates a willingness to assist the helpee in the exploration. The wording for use in open-ended questions will need to be taught as well as the use of the questions.

The closed question tends to cut off the dialogue by emphasizing factual content rather than feelings. The closed question usually can be answered by a yes or no or with a few words. The helpee often feels when a closed question is asked by the helper that the helper lacks interest in the helpee.

Training Procedures

1. Discuss differences between open-ended and closed questions.

2. Model open-ended and closed questions. Also show how questions can be used for different purposes. Some purposes and examples are provided in Exercise 8.1 in the *Peer Power, Book One, Workbook.*

   Optional: Use video equipment to show previously prepared video of open-ended and closed questions.

3. Have trainees share and discuss examples of their open-ended and closed questions that they prepared in Exercise 8.1.

4. Discuss trainees' concerns about open-ended questions and their use.

5. Collect Exercise 8.1 sheets.

6. Return Exercise 7.2 sheets (also 7.1 sheets if not previously returned) with written comments.

Application for Trainees After the Group Meeting

If not previously done, ask trainees to read and be prepared to complete Exercise 8.2 in the next group meeting.

EXERCISE 8.2
IDENTIFYING GOOD QUESTIONS

Goal

To provide experience for the trainees in recognizing good questions

Time Needed—Trainees' preparation: 15 to 30 minutes for this exercise
Group work: 30 to 45 minutes

Introduction to the Exercise

First recognize both good questions and poor ones. This exercise can either be used as an application or be done during the training time and discussed as the trainees mark their responses.

Training Procedures

1. Ask the trainees to read and rate each question.
2. Have the trainer rate each question in terms of poor, fair, good, and excellent.
3. Have trainees check the appropriate place.

Application for Trainees After the Group Meeting

Have trainees review Exercise 8.3 and come prepared for the next group meeting to do as stated in the directions.

EXERCISE 8.3
RATING THE HELPER

Goal

To provide experience for the trainees in using and rating open-ended questions

Time Needed—Trainees' preparation: 10 to 20 minutes for this exercise
Group work: 0 to 45 minutes

Introduction to the Exercise

Trainees need an opportunity to practice the open-ended questioning skill. While doing so, they should continue using other skills where and when appropriate. Exercise 8.2 is designed to provide this experience and to have trainees assist one another in learning and improving skills. An example is provided of an extended dialogue using open-ended questions and empathy. Trainees can study the example to be prepared for role-playing during the training session.

Training Procedures

1. Answer any questions the trainees have regarding the directions given for Exercise 8.3.

2. Have trainees do practice in triads and have them complete the Rating Flow Sheet.

3. Move from cluster to cluster and assist where necessary.

   Optional: Video one or more of the clusters during role-play and replay the tape for trainees.

4. After each extended dialogue is practiced, discuss what occurred and assist trainees in completing the Rating Flow Sheet.

5. Collect Exercise 8.3 sheets.

6. If application time existed between Exercises 8.1 and 8.3, then return Exercise 8.1 sheets with written comments. If no application time was available, retain Exercise 8.1 sheets to be returned later.

Application for Trainees After the Group Meeting

1. Ask trainees to do Exercise 8.4 and submit the completed sheets to you.

2. Ask trainees to review the introductory comments to Module IX.

3. Ask trainees to study the information supplied in Exercise 9.1 and complete the exercise sheets before the next training session.

4. If Exercises 9.1, 9.2, and 9.3 are to be covered in the same training session, ask the trainees to study and complete

Exercise 9.2 at home. They should study Exercise 9.3 but should leave the exercise sheets to be completed during the next training session.

EXERCISE 8.4
DIARY

Goal

To have trainees practice their questioning skill with friends

Time Needed—Trainees' preparation: no time needed for this exercise

Group work: possibly no time, or an option of 15 to 60 minutes for review and practice of skill

Introduction to the Exercise

The exercise consists of activities to be done outside the training session to provide the trainees practice with the questioning skill. No training session time is needed unless the trainer wants to have the trainees discuss their experiences and use the feedback to decide whether or not additional training is needed.

Training Procedures

1. Following completion of Exercise 8.3, have trainees do Exercise 8.4 outside the training session.

2. If feedback is desired to determine competencies of trainees, discuss Exercise 8.4 sheets in the next training session. Provide opportunities for trainees to improve their competencies in skills taught thus far before continuing in the workbook.

3. Collect Exercise 8.4 sheets at the training session immediately following their assignment.

4. If training session time is used for Exercise 8.4, return Exercises 8.1 and 8.3 sheets with written comments.

Application for Trainees After the Group Meeting

1. Continuation of assignment made as an application at close of Exercise 8.3.

2. Ask trainees to complete the notes for this module and discuss in the training group their reaction to the skill. Discuss how this applies to their daily lives.

MODULE **IX**

GENUINENESS SKILL

INTRODUCTION

In Module IX the major focus is on genuine responses. The trainees are to be taught how they can share their own feelings about what the helpee is saying or doing and maintain or enhance the relationship by doing so. By enabling the trainees to learn genuineness skill, they can express their feelings rather than concealing feelings or becoming aggressive.

In addition to learning about nonresponsive, nongenuine, and genuine responses, the trainees will be asked to use the other skills also. Opportunities for experience are to be provided for the trainees to integrate all five peer helping skills taught in the training sessions thus far.

The number of training sessions will depend upon your situation and the abilities of the trainees. The recommendation is for a minimum of three training sessions with the exercise grouped as shown on the chart in this session; however, the exercises are each self-contained and can be grouped together differently or taught one in each session.

Trainees who are introverted may have a difficult time with this module.

Goal

To enable trainees to learn about, recognize, and use genuineness skill

Time Needed—Trainees' preparation: 2½ to 3½ hours for nine exercises
Group work: 2¾ to 4¼ hours for nine exercises

Materials

- *Peer Power, Book One, Workbook* (one for each trainee)
- Flip chart paper or whiteboard
- Pencil or pen for each trainee
- Name tag for name on shirt
- Sticky notes for trainees to utilize during training
- Snacks for trainees if budget permits
- Crayons
- Koosh balls or other things to hold in their hands
- Rewards to give to trainees at appropriate times (M&M's, etc.)
- Optional: Video equipment with previously produced video containing one or more examples of the behavior being taught
- Optional: CD to play music to bring trainees together (you may want to have a theme song or music by this time such as "Lean on Me" or other appropriate music agreed upon by the group)
- Audio recorder for each triad

Suggested Grouping of Exercises by Training Sessions

First session: complete Exercises 9.1, 9.2, and 9.3

Second session: complete Exercises 9.4, 9.5, and 9.6

Third session: complete Exercises 9.7 and 9.8 with Exercise 9.9 to be done outside of training session

Training Procedures

1. Decide on grouping of exercises for the training sessions. The decision will make a difference in application assignments and the time available for each exercise.

2. Follow the sequence of exercises and training procedures for each.

3. Move from cluster to cluster during practicing to identify points that need additional emphases and perhaps to identify individual trainees who may require additional assistance, maybe even outside of the regular training program.

4. Arrange for audio or video recording and playback. The trainees can gain much from seeing and/or hearing themselves. The feedback by trainer and trainee-raters can be facilitated by tape playback.

EXERCISE 9.1
A COMPARISON OF NONRESPONSIVE, NONGENUINE, AND GENUINE RESPONSES

Goal

To enable trainees to differentiate among the three kinds of responses—nonresponsive, nongenuine, and genuine—and to understand the feelings generally prompted in the person to whom the response is made

Time Needed—Trainees' preparation: 60 to 90 minutes for this exercise
Group work: 30 to 45 minutes

Introduction to the Exercise

This exercise is designed to help trainees learn the differences among the three kinds of responses. By increasing their awareness and by having them prepare responses for different situations, they should be better able to use genuine responses with other people.

Learning the differences among the three kinds of responses may not be easy for some trainees. Examples and demonstrations will need to be given to enable trainees to understand the importance of genuine responses. Placing the trainees into situations that cause them to make and/or receive different responses will assist them in gaining an understanding of the feelings generally caused in the person to whom the response is made.

1. Introduce genuineness skill by discussing different ways that a person lets others know about personal feelings.

2. Ask each trainee to discuss how he/she communicates anger, irritation, and so forth.

3. After trainees are discussing freely, have trainees determine how they handle anger by using the "Chart of Feelings During Three Kinds of Response Behaviors" for reference. The chart is in Exercise 9.1 in *Peer Power, Book One.*

4. As trainer, demonstrate different ways of initiating interchange concerning the helpee's feelings.

   Situation: The trainee plays the role of a person criticizing his/her brother. The trainer reads the following statements without telling which kind is going to be illustrated.

   a. Nonresponsive Response

      Trainer: "You must really like your brother."

      Trainee Response: "No, he really irritates me."

      Trainer requests that the group identify from the previous dialogue which of the three levels of genuineness the trainer's response modeled. Trainer repeats modeling responses, using examples of nonresponsive responses, until trainees understand how to identify nonresponsive behavior.

   b. Nongenuine Response

      Trainer models the nongenuine behavior using the same situation.

      Trainer: "You made a dumb statement about your brother."

      Trainee Response: "Well, he is dumb! If you only knew."

      Trainer repeats the two steps.

c. Genuine Response

Trainer models the genuine response using the same situation.

> Trainer: "When you criticize your brother, I feel uneasy and just want to leave the room."

> Trainee Response: "Well, I'm not mad at him; I just get upset with him."

Trainer repeats the two steps.

5. As trainer, initiate a helper statement after which a trainee is asked to respond with feeling. The other trainees then identify which kind of genuineness is reported by the trainee (nonresponsive, nongenuine, or genuine). Repeat the process several times.

Optional: Introduce a practicing situation in which one says the following:

"I, the trainer, will go around the room in progression and make a series of statements, requesting a response from each trainee. As you hear the statement by the trainer and response by a trainee, the rest of you in the group are to decide the following three things:

(1) Will the relationship be maintained as the result of the statement by me?

(2) Is there a good chance that the offending person, the trainee, will change his/her behavior?

(3) Was I, the person who sent the message, honest with my feelings?"

Then state the practicing situation:

"I have invited all of you to my house to listen to music. I have a new white carpet, and all of you have muddy shoes."

Next make the following statement to a trainee you select to give a response:

"You dummy, didn't your mother teach you any differently than to walk on carpet with muddy feet!"

a. Response from a trainee.

b. Then ask the other group members, "Does the trainee response meet the three conditions?"

Repeat the last process by making the following statement to a trainee chosen to give the response.

"Let me tell you a joke about a kid that was inconsiderate to his friend..."

    a. Response from a trainee.

    b. Then ask the other group members, "Does the trainee response meet the three conditions?"

Discuss the trainees' comments and help them work with their concerns.

6. Collect Exercises 8.3 (if not previously collected) and 9.1.

7. Return exercise sheets that have not previously been returned. These may include 8.1, 8.2, and 8.3.

Application for Trainees After the Group Meeting

1. If Exercise 9.2 is not covered in the same training session as 9.1, then ask trainees to study and complete Exercise 9.2 before the next session.

2. If Exercise 9.2 is covered in the same training session as 9.1, then give no applications between 9.1 and 9.2 because 9.2 should have been completed before the start of training session.

EXERCISE 9.2
HOW OPEN AM I?

Goal

To increase trainees' awareness of how open they are and with whom

Time Needed—Trainees' preparation: 30 to 45 minutes for this exercise
                Group work: 10 to 20 minutes

Introduction to the Exercise

The openness one has may depend on several things including the situation, the topic, and the person or persons with whom one is sharing. This exercise is designed to cause trainees to think about what they would share and with whom they would share which kinds of topics.

The closeness in a relationship may increase the willingness to discuss a topic. After the trainees have recorded their topics with each of four kinds of persons, they are asked to mark their openness on a Likert-type scale.

Training Procedures

1. Discuss with the trainees the purpose of Exercise 9.2.
2. Have trainees share their feelings and comments from preparing Exercise 9.2.
3. Have trainees discuss the differences in kinds of topics discussed.
4. When trainees are discussing freely, move on to Exercise 9.3.

Application for Trainees After the Group Meeting

Have them read Exercise 9.3 and come prepared to complete it during the next group meeting.

EXERCISE 9.3
OPENNESS CIRCLE

Goal

To cause trainees to examine further the extent of their openness and with whom

Time Needed—Trainees' preparation: 0 to 5 minutes for this
exercise
Group work: 10 to 20 minutes

Introduction to the Exercise

The form for doing the Openness Circle Game is provided in Exercise 9.3, *Peer Power, Book One, Workbook.* All of the directions are provided in the following section entitled, "Training Procedures." The game is one that often stimulates trainees' thinking and produces much discussion. The result may cause trainees to examine their own values and openness. Also, trainees may better understand the people with whom they work and their reluctance to discuss some topics and not others.

Training Procedures

1. Ask trainees to open *Peer Power, Book One, Workbook* to Exercise 9.3 and prepare to complete the circle as you give them directions (each trainee will need a writing instrument).

2. Explain the meaning of each of the circles as follows:

   a. **Intimates Circle**—feelings and experiences I share with my closest friend(s) (could be family).

   b. **Friends Circle**—feelings and experiences I share with the group with which I spend time.

   c. **Acquaintances Circle**—feelings and experiences I share with people I know casually.

   d. **Strangers Circle**—feelings and experiences I share with people with whom I am not acquainted.

3. Review with the trainees what was learned in Exercise 9.2, which generally is that a closed person would share most of his/her feelings and experiences with only intimates. The more open a person is, the more feelings and experiences that person shares with friends, acquaintances, and strangers.

4. Ask the following series of questions and have trainees write the keyword from the question on the appropriate area in the circle representing with whom they would share the following information.

   a. With whom would you share the fact that you have shoplifted?

   b. With whom would you share the fact that you have smoked marijuana?

c. With whom would you share the fact that you plagia-rized a paper for school?

d. With whom would you share a deep, personal problem?

e. With whom would you share a physical problem?

f. With whom would you share two things you do well?

g. With whom would you share two bad things about yourself?

5. Ask each trainee to tell how many items were placed in each category of the circle. Record number of items on a large set of circles on chalkboard or flipchart so that train-ees can understand how their own circle compares with the composite of all trainees.

6. Ask the group to determine who is most closed and open in relationships with others according to placement of topics on circle.

7. Ask the most open and most closed trainees to stand at opposite ends of the room, which represents the extremes of the circle, with an area for those who are somewhat open or closed in the middle, then ask trainees to position them-selves between the two extremes by talking with persons standing next to them to compare circles. As the result of the comparison, one trainee may find he/she is more open or closed than the person with whom he/she is talk-ing. If so, change places to represent the newly interpreted position.

8. Point out that those trainees who see themselves as closed may have to work harder at being genuine.

9. Discuss the concerns the trainees have about openness.

10. Collect Exercises 9.2 and 9.3.

11. Return Exercises 8.3 (if not previously returned) and 9.1 with written comments.

Application for Trainees After the Group Meeting

1. Ask trainees to study Exercise 9.4, then prepare the genu-ine message requested, and come to the next training ses-sion prepared to complete the exercise.

2. If Exercise 9.5 is to be covered in the next training session, ask trainees to review it and come prepared to do the practicing during the training session.

3. If Exercise 9.6 is to be covered in the next training session, ask the trainees to complete it before the next session.

EXERCISE 9.4
PUTTING TOGETHER A GENUINE MESSAGE

Goal

To have trainees examine in greater detail the contents of a genuine message and then practice making and analyzing genuine messages

Time Needed—Trainees' preparation: 10 to 15 minutes for this exercise
Group work: 30 to 40 minutes

Introduction to the Exercise

The genuine message is sent with an "I" message as opposed to a "you" (nongenuine) message. The four parts of the genuine message are described in *Peer Power, Book One, Workbook,* Exercise 9.4, with an example developed to identify the parts. In addition, a communication model for the helper to use in putting together a genuine message is provided.

Exercise 9.4 is a means to have trainees examine in greater detail the contents of genuine messages. Space is provided for writing a genuine message with the four parts, and space in chart form is provided to analyze two genuine messages, one from the trainer and one written by another trainee.

Training Procedures

1. Discuss the four parts of the genuine message as outlined in Exercise 9.4, *Peer Power, Book One, Workbook* and work with the concerns expressed by trainees.

2. Give illustrations of genuine messages and identify the four parts on chalkboard or flip chart in the same manner as trainees are to record in chart form in Exercise 9.4. Have trainees participate in identifying the four parts.

3. Give the following statement and ask trainees to record the four parts in the space provided in their Exercise 9.4 chart.

Situation: A friend borrowed $50 a week ago and has not paid it back or made any arrangements to pay it back. An example of genuineness in responding would be: "I am really disappointed in you for not paying me back the $50 or letting me know when you would pay me back and that makes me very hesitant to ever loan you money again because I can't depend on your paying it back."

Check trainees' recordings, which would resemble the following:

How I feel	—really disappointed
What has happened	—not paying
How this affects me	—makes me very hesitant
Reason	—can't depend on you

4. Place the trainees in clusters of two and ask them to follow Directions 5, 6, and 7 on Exercise 9.4 sheets.

5. Discuss any concerns the trainees have following their work in clusters.

6. Collect Exercise 9.4 sheets.

7. Return Exercises 9.2 and 9.3 sheets with written comments.

Application for Trainees After the Group Meeting

The application assignment depends upon the grouping of exercises to be covered in each training session. If Exercises 9.5 and 9.6 are covered in the same session as 9.4, they should have been assigned previously. If not, assign them for the next session.

EXERCISE 9.5
WHEN TO USE A GENUINE MESSAGE

Goal

To provide trainees with experience through practice using genuine messages

Time Needed—Trainees' preparation: 0 to 5 minutes for this exercise
Group work: 15 to 30 minutes

Introduction to the Exercise

Exercise 9.5 requires training session time to practice but does not require note taking or prior written work. The trainees need to read the exercise and be prepared to do it. The entire purpose is to provide experience for the trainees to use genuine messages in the training session where the trainer can observe their proficiency and identify points that may need additional emphases.

Training Procedures

1. Discuss with the trainees the purpose of the exercise and what the trainer will be doing during their practicing.

2. Cluster trainees in dyads and ask them to follow the directions in Exercise 9.5, *Peer Power, Book One, Workbook*.

   Optional: View and discuss a video demonstrating the roles described in Exercise 9.5.

3. Stop the practice after a short time to discuss trainees' concerns and to share with them what was learned by moving from dyad to dyad.

4. Close the exercise with a discussion of their experiences and concerns.

5. Tell the trainees that no exercise sheets are to be submitted since no written material was prepared for Exercise 9.5.

Application for Trainees After the Group Meeting

Have trainees study and complete Exercise 9.6 before the next group meeting.

EXERCISE 9.6
PRACTICE SENDING GENUINE RESPONSES

Goal

To give trainees experience in writing genuine messages

Time Needed—Trainees' preparation: 5 to 10 minutes for this exercise
Group work: 10 to 15 minutes

Introduction to the Exercise

This exercise enables trainees to study a situation and a nongenuine message and then develop a genuine message. This exercise reviews earlier material and practices and enables the trainer to evaluate from written material whether or not the trainees are learning the behavior.

Training Procedures

1. Have trainees discuss their genuine messages written for Exercise 9.6. The genuine messages might be similar to the following:

   a. Situation 1: "I had to make special arrangements to go to the movies at the time you suggested. I feel you just take me for granted, that I can have the car anytime, and I don't feel like going through the hassle to go to the later showing."

   b. Situation 2: "I get irritated when you keep bugging me about keeping my room clean without considering my brother's part. I feel like moving my brother out because I get so mad at him."

c. Situation 3: "I feel so bad since you have been avoiding me for the last few days. It is really frustrating not being able to see you like I used to."

d. Situation 4: "I was wondering if I upset you because you haven't talked to me in a week. I have been worried."

2. Discuss any concerns the trainees still have regarding genuine responses, and do the additional training that may be needed to bring their proficiency up to expected level.

3. Collect Exercise 9.6 sheets.

4. Return any exercise sheets that were collected in a previous training session but have not been returned.

Application for Trainees After the Group Meeting

1. Ask trainees to prepare for the next training session and to complete the application where requested in those exercises that will be covered in the next training session. The suggestion is to cover Exercises 9.7 and 9.8 during the next session.

2. Exercise 9.9 is to be done outside of the training session. It may be assigned to do before doing 9.7 and 9.8 in training session so as to discuss it along with 9.7 and 9.8.

EXERCISE 9.7
UNDERSTANDING HOW GENUINENESS IS USED

Goal

To have trainees use empathic and genuineness responses in appropriate situations

Time Needed—Trainees' preparation: 10 to 15 minutes for this exercise
Group work: 30 to 45 minutes

Introduction to the Exercise

Exercise 9.7 enables the trainees to study more about genuineness responses and to use them along with empathy responses. Examples are provided including an extended dialogue with analysis.

Trainees are to practice and rate each other so as to provide meaningful feedback for their development. The trainer will be able to learn much about their development by moving from cluster to cluster and assisting where needed.

Exercises 9.7 and 9.8 may be done in the same training session if trainees are making good progress. If trainees are learning slowly or are having difficulty, the suggestion is that a time period should elapse between the two exercises.

Training Procedures

1. Demonstrate the empathy and genuineness responses by means of a dialogue with one of the trainees.

   Optional: Use video equipment to show the behavior desired and stop the video at different places to emphasize various points. Have the trainees take an active role in the discussion.

2. Discuss with the trainees their concerns about doing Exercise 9.7.

3. Cluster the trainees in triads and ask them to complete Exercise 9.7 according to the directions in their workbooks with the additional verbal directions the trainer will provide. Have a means of either audio or video recording each triad's practice round.

4. Assign roles to helpee, helper, and rater, and ask helper to establish the situation by describing the role function that the helpee will initiate (behavior that bothers helper). Ask rater to record the practice interchanges.

5. Ask helpee to demonstrate the behavior, and ask helper to respond with four dimensions of genuineness skill (true feelings, specific happenings, reasons, and effects).

6. Ask the helper to give a genuineness communication and then to follow the helpee's next statement with high-level empathy responses.

7. Tell helper that he/she may choose to continue empathic responses or alternate empathic and genuineness responses. Goals of the helper at this point will be the resolution of the relationship difficulties and maintaining or improving the relationship.

8. During the triad practice and discussion, tell the trainees that the trainer will move from cluster to cluster to observe and facilitate practice. Following the triad discussion groups, the trainer will participate in the feedback experience.

9. After the first practice interchanges, have the rater play back the tape and stop it at various places. The rater is to ask helpee and helper to describe feelings at the stopping point of the tape. Suggest possible rater questions such as the following:

   a. What were your feelings when the helper gave you a genuine response?

   b. How did you (helpee) feel at this point in the interchange?

   c. What behavior did you (helpee) want the helper to show?

10. The rater is also to complete the Rating Flow Sheet provided in Exercise 9.7 in *Peer Power, Book One, Workbook.*

11. Reverse roles until everyone has had a chance to play each role and an opportunity to tape each set of interchanges and discuss them.

12. Discuss any concerns the trainees have.

13. Collect Exercise 9.7 sheets.

14. Return any exercise sheets collected in previous training sessions.

Application for Trainees After the Group Meeting

1. If Exercise 9.8 has not been assigned, ask trainees to review it and be prepared to complete the Rating Flow Sheet in the next training session.

2. Ask trainees to review and complete Exercise 9.9 before the next training session if it has not been assigned previously.

EXERCISE 9.8
INTEGRATING COMMUNICATION SKILLS

Goal

To provide practice for trainees in integrating their attending, empathy, questioning, summarizing, and genuineness skills

Time Needed—Trainees' preparation: 0 to 5 minutes for this exercise
Group work: 30 to 45 minutes

Introduction to the Exercise

Exercise 9.8 follows well on Exercise 9.7 and may be done in the same training session. The trainees have learned five communication skills and need the opportunity to practice using all of them, if appropriate, in an extended dialogue. The experience is provided in Exercise 9.8 with other trainees during a training session so that the trainer can obtain feedback on what needs to be done to increase the trainees' skills.

Training Procedures

1. Discuss with trainees what the purpose of the exercise is and answer any questions they have.

2. Cluster the trainees in triads and ask them to take the roles of helpee, helper, and rater.

3. Ask the helpee to take a situation in which he/she can play a role for an extended interchange.

4. Ask the helper to use the appropriate communication response and to try to use the skills of attending, empathy, open-ended questioning, and genuineness.

5. Ask the rater to complete during role-playing the Rating Flow Sheet for Integrating Communication Skills in *Peer Power, Book One, Workbook*, Exercise 9.8.

   Optional: Ask the rater to record the practice exercise and to use the recording during feedback given by the rater.

6. Move from triad to triad and assist where needed plus observe and listen for points that need to be emphasized.

7. At the end of the first practice round and feedback, discuss as a total group the concerns of the trainees.

8. Repeat two more times the previous procedures with the trainees changing roles so that each has played all three.

9. Collect Exercise 9.8 sheets.

10. Return any exercise sheets collected in prior training sessions that have not been returned previously.

Application for Trainees After the Group Meeting

1. If Exercise 9.9 has not been assigned previously, ask the trainees to complete it prior to the next training session.

2. Ask trainees to study the introductory material to Module X and then study and complete Exercises 10.1 and 10.2 before the next training session.

EXERCISE 9.9
USING GENUINE RESPONSES

Goal

To make trainees aware of opportunities for them to use their communication skills in everyday life and to have them record the genuine responses used between training sessions

Time Needed—Trainees' preparation: 15 to 20 minutes for this exercise
Group work: none required

Introduction to the Exercise

As stated in the purpose, the exercise is a means to have trainees consider opportunities for them to use their improved and new skills in everyday life. Since Module IX was devoted to genuine responses, the trainees are asked to record the genuine responses between the two training sessions.

The exercise sheets offer the trainer an excellent means of determining how well the trainees have mastered the skill, the kinds of conditions in which they use the skill, and which trainees may need special attention. Written comments by the trainer on the exercise sheets can be a way of reinforcing the good practices of the trainees and of calling their attention to behaviors that require additional effort.

Training Procedures

1. Have Exercise 9.9 completed between training sessions.

2. If training is not progressing rapidly, use time in the next training session to discuss the trainees' experiences, their concerns, and their written comments.

3. Collect Exercise 9.9 sheets at the next training session.

4. Request that the trainees complete the notes section at the end of Module IX. Ask for two volunteers to share their reactions.

MODULE

ASSERTIVENESS SKILL

INTRODUCTION

In Module X the major focus is on assertion, awareness, and assertive responses. The trainees are taught the differences among assertive, nonassertive, and aggressive communication. They also will be asked to decide in which relationships they would like to become more assertive. They are asked to keep a daily log, which is very important in helping them recognize how they are communicating.

The trainees also are asked to practice assertive skills. Assertiveness is actually an extension of genuineness and an integral part of openness and confrontation.

Goals

To enable trainees to learn about, recognize, and use assertiveness skills

To help trainees learn assertiveness skills, both verbal and nonverbal, through the exercises and practice

Time Needed—Trainees' preparation: 1½ to 3½ hours for six exercises

Group work: 3¼ to 4½ hours for six exercises

Materials

- *Peer Power, Book One, Workbook* (one for each trainee)
- Flip chart paper or whiteboard
- Pencil or pen for each trainee
- Name tag for name on shirt
- Sticky notes for trainees to utilize during training
- Snacks for trainees if budget permits
- Crayons
- Koosh balls or other things to hold in their hands
- Rewards to give to trainees at appropriate times (M&M's, etc.)
- Optional: Video equipment with previously produced video containing one or more examples of the behavior being taught
- Optional: CD player to play music to bring trainees together (you may want to have a theme song or music by this time such as "Lean on Me" or other appropriate music agreed upon by the group)
- Audio recorder for every triad

Training Procedures

1. Decide on the grouping of exercises for the training sessions. The decision will affect the preparation and application assignments.
2. Follow the sequence of exercises and the Training Procedures for each.
3. Move from cluster to cluster during the practice time to identify points that need additional emphases and to identify individual trainees who may require special assistance, perhaps outside of the regular training program.
4. Carefully read the logs and give written and verbal feedback to the trainees.

5. Arrange for audio or video recording and playback. The trainees can gain much from seeing and hearing themselves. The feedback by trainer and trainee-raters can be facilitated by replay.

6. Assertive behavior may be acquired by watching others model assertive responses. Modeling has an informative function; it shows group members how to be assertive; it gives them permission to behave similarly; it provides information about the consequences of such behavior; it strengthens existing assertive behavior; and it establishes new skills in assertion.

For example, watching the trainer model refusing an unreasonable request tells the group members, "This is an unreasonable request" (and helps them to discriminate between reasonable and unreasonable requests). It tells the group what verbal and nonverbal behaviors are appropriate. It shows the trainees how to make the response and lets them know that it is okay to stand up for one's rights.

Modeling, therefore, produces learning primarily through the dissemination and retention of information. The observers characterize the modeled event symbolically in the form of images and verbal codes, and they store this information for future use (Bandura, 2006).

Note that attention is a necessary prerequisite for learning through modeling. The observer must recognize, differentiate, and attend to the distinctive features of the model's responses (Bandura, 1995). Several factors can influence an observer's responsiveness to modeling influences.

Research has shown that the most effective models are persons who are highly competent and who have prestige and status. This finding suggested that facilitators (because of their roles and skills) exert a considerable impact upon group members. It also provides another reason to emphasize the need for facilitators to be good role models.

In conclusion, it is important to note that the retention of modeled responses is greatly strengthened when the observer has the opportunity to rehearse and practice the modeled behavior.

7. As you begin to train others in assertiveness, keep in mind the type preferences of members of your training group. In general, females that have a preference for Extroversion, Intuitiveness, and Thinking tend to be more assertive. For males the Extroverted are more assertive. Specific types including E, N, ENTJ, ENTP, ENFJ, and ESTJ report more assertiveness than I, S, ISFP, ISFJ, INFP, and ISTP (Williams & Bukemiller, 1992). You may need to work with your introverted females and males to help them express themselves. Remember, Introverts tend to keep things to themselves.

8. You might want to ask these general questions as a motivator to start this module.

   a. Do you ask for help when you need help?

   b. Do you express anger in a way that does not put others off?

   c. Do you ask questions when you don't understand?

   d. Do you volunteer your opinions when you think differently from others?

   e. Do you speak up in a meeting or class often?

   f. Are you able to say "no" if you can't or don't want to do something and another person has asked you to do it?

   g. Do you look at people when you are speaking?

   h. Do you speak in a confident manner?

   Emphasize that by being assertive you may feel somewhat unpleasant for a while, but in the long run, your relationship with the other person will be strengthened.

9. Practice is a learning-by-doing strategy and a key focus in the assertiveness training. Practice may be defined as the behavioral enactment of an interpersonal encounter, but role-play involves more than merely acting out a scene. It encompasses a behavioral rehearsal of "those specific assertive responses which are to become part of their behavioral repertoire" (Jakubowski-Spencer, 1973a).

   Role-playing (practice) facilitates the acquisition of assertiveness behavior because it allows the group to practice their assertive skills in a safe environment. It provides valuable information about the assertive role-player's behavior through self-observation and the observation of others. It strengthens self-confidence as well as assertiveness skills. It permits group members to learn from watching each other.

Group members are asked to volunteer incidents that have happened to them in the past or that they think will happen to them in the future.

10. Processing is one way of maximizing the effectiveness of group exercise. It involves taking a close look at what each individual has experienced and how group members interact with each other. The goals of processing are to encourage self-evaluation, to provide a mechanism by which feelings about self and others are shared, to encourage the individual to take risks, to aid in the acquisition of assertiveness skills, and to help develop feelings of trust and closeness.

Processing can most easily be implemented by asking group members to focus on their feelings, observations, and thoughts and to share them honestly and directly with the group.

Evaluation Process

As trainer, evaluate the process used in teaching assertive behavior skills by the feedback obtained from the trainees and by observations of the trainees' written work and their behavior during the sessions.

Measuring Outcomes

1. Use Exercises 10.1, 10.2, and 10.3 to identify the trainees' assertiveness skills.

2. Use Exercise 10.4 to evaluate how they are incorporating assertion into their daily lives.

3. Observe and listen during the role-playing in Exercises 10.5 and 10.6 to measure the ease with which trainees are using assertiveness in their lives.

EXERCISE 10.1
DIFFERENCES AMONG ASSERTIVE, NONASSERTIVE, AND AGGRESSIVE BEHAVIORS

Goal

To help trainees learn the differences among these three important types of behavior and when it is appropriate to use each different style of communication

Time Needed—Trainees' preparation: 30 to 45 minutes for this exercise

Group work: 30 to 45 minutes

Introduction to the Exercise

This exercise is designed to help trainees learn the difference among the three kinds of responses. By increasing their awareness and by having them prepare responses for different situations, they should be better able to use assertive responses with other persons.

Learning the differences among these kinds of responses may not be easy for some trainees. Examples and demonstrations should be given to enable them to understand the importance of assertiveness in responses. Placing the trainees into activities that cause them to make and/or receive different responses will assist them in gaining an understanding of the feelings generally caused in the person to whom the response is made.

Training Procedures

1. Ask the trainees to read the material before the training session begins.

2. Ask the trainees when they are assertive, nonassertive, and aggressive. You may want to place signs on different parts of the room (Assertive, Nonassertive, Aggressive). Ask trainees to go to the signs that represent their natural way of communication. Ask them in their small groups to give

examples. Next, ask them to move to the sign that they would like to be.

3. Ask the trainees to discuss how significant others behave toward them (parents, teachers, bosses, and so forth).

4. Ask the trainees to discuss how they communicate anger, needs, and so forth.

Situation: *Someone has borrowed my fur coat to wear to a dance but has not returned it.*

Aggressive—"You are being really inconsiderate by not bringing back my coat. If you can't be more considerate, I don't want to be your friend anymore."

Nonassertive—says nothing about the coat.

Assertive—"I'm worried about my coat. You promised to bring it back last week and still haven't. Please bring it back today because I need it to wear to a dance."

5. Have each person in the group think about times when they behaved in an aggressive, nonassertive, and assertive manner. What were their feelings and what were the results? The leader may want to model an example.

Examples

a. Assertive—"I took back a dress that did not have good workmanship. The owner did not want it back, but I was firm about the fact that I had shopped there many times and rarely returned anything."

Feelings: confidence.

Result: The owner returned my money.

b. Nonassertive—"My neighbor asked me to watch her small child. I was busy, but I said yes."

Feelings: Anger.

Result: Cool toward neighbor and frustrated because I was so busy.

c. Aggressive—"I yelled at my coworker for not finishing a project on time."

Feelings: Justified at the time and guilty afterward.

Result: The project was completed, but the coworker would not speak to me.

6. Have the trainees name instances when someone else was aggressive, nonassertive, and assertive. How did they feel, and what were the results?

Application for Trainees After the Group Meeting

1. Have trainees complete Exercise 10.2 before the next group meeting.

2. Ask them to listen to others and identify assertive messages.

EXERCISE 10.2
MY ASSERTIVENESS PROFILE

Goal

To increase the trainees' awareness of how assertive they are in what kinds of situations

Time Needed—Trainees' preparation: 15 to 30 minutes for this exercise
Group work: 15 to 30 minutes

Introduction to the Exercise

The assertiveness questions are designed to help trainees think about when they are assertive. They are asked to indicate if they display this behavior almost always, sometimes, or rarely.

Training Procedures

1. Collect homework from Exercise 10.1. Make written comments and return.

2. If the trainees did not take home the profile, ask them to fill it out now.

3. Ask the trainees to follow the directions to score their profile.

4. Have them mark their score on the Assertiveness Scale.

5. Have the trainees share their scores with the group. Have them share what type of activities affected their scores.

6. Have them discuss in what situations and with whom they are most nonassertive.

Application for Trainees After the Group Meeting

1. Ask trainees to complete Exercise 10.3 before the next group meeting.

2. Ask them to think about how the results on the profile are demonstrated in their daily life.

EXERCISE 10.3
WHEN SHOULD I BE ASSERTIVE?

Goal

To assist trainees in further refining their skills in identifying situations in which they want to be more assertive

Time Needed—Trainees' preparation: 15 to 30 minutes for this exercise
Group work: 10 to 20 minutes

Training Procedures

1. Ask for any feedback they may have from Exercise 10.2.

2. If trainees have completed Exercise 10.3, they can discuss the results using the following suggestions:

   a. Look at the overall questionnaire and identify those areas that threatened you. Why did they?

   b. Look at your list and think about making some changes to become more assertive.

Application for Trainees After the Group Meeting

1. Have trainees complete Exercise 10.4, which can be done before the next group meeting.

2. Attempt to use assertive skill with family or friends and notice feedback.

EXERCISE 10.4
DAILY LOG

Goal

To help trainees further refine areas in which they want to make changes and to keep a daily log of situations in which they were assertive

Time Needed—Trainees' preparation: 30 to 45 minutes for this exercise
Group work: 45 to 60 minutes

Introduction to the Exercise

The areas that will be used to develop the scenes for role-playing will be from Exercise 10.3. Ask the trainees to be very specific about their scenes. Ask them to role-play some of the scenes. This is the best way to begin to become more assertive. The trainees also will be asked to start keeping a log.

Training Procedures

1. Ask the trainees to review their scenes as written for Direction 1 in the workbook.

2. Have them include the following components:

   a. The person involved

   b. When it takes place (time and setting)

   c. What bothers you

   d. How you deal with the situation

e. Fear of what will happen

f. Goal (what you would like to see happen)

3. Assist the trainees in helping each other revise, if necessary, the scenes to include all of the components.

4. Ask the trainees to role-play some of the scenes.

5. Suggested procedure for role-playing:

  a. Ask if anyone has a situation or scene on which he/she would like to work (Trainee #1).

  b. Ask Trainee #1 to briefly describe the scene, reading the description just written. This will permit others to play the scene.

  c. Ask if Volunteer #1 would like to play either part.

  d. Suggest that the practice begin and encourage the other group members to observe. Ask the observers to state what went well and what could have gone better.

  e. Upon completion of the practice, ask the trainees to share their feelings and observations about the encounter. Ask the observers to give their comments and observations, and then offer your own observations. It is important that the trainer praise all approximations of assertive behavior and give focused suggestions for improvement.

  f. The trainer may then have the different trainees play the same scene or have the original trainees change roles.

  g. Once Trainee #1 has demonstrated adequate assertiveness skills with this situation, the role-play may be repeated and made more difficult by instructing Trainee #2 to behave in an uncooperative manner.

  h. Some group members may initially be reluctant to engage in role-playing and may require the trainer's assistance. In role-playing, it is possible for a group member to "get stuck." In such a case, the trainer may need to coach the role-player, provide additional encouragement, suggest a role reversal, or break the role-play situation into smaller units.

6. Have trainees break into groups of three, read their scenes, practice role-playing, and get feedback from the observer.

7. Ask students to maintain a log for the next few days and turn it in to the trainer for comment.

8. Explain that the log is similar to a diary; it is a written description of interpersonal encounters. It should include the individual's perception of what happened, with whom, feelings at the time and afterwards, and the consequences. The purpose of the log is to:

    a. Increase awareness of the individual's behavior and relationships with others

    b. Help identify situations and individuals with whom the person had difficulty in interpersonal encounters

    c. Serve as a progress chart to show the individual's development

    d. Allow for additional feedback from the trainer

9. Group members will turn in their logs at the beginning of the next two training meetings. The task of the trainer is to read each log carefully and provide comments. These comments may take several forms.

    a. Rewarding: Praise all successful attempts at assertion, even small ones.

    b. Encouraging: Show support, understanding, and appreciation for their insights, frustrations, and unsuccessful attempts at assertion.

    c. Challenging: Ask the trainees to think of alternatives.

    d. Confronting: Point out discrepancies.

    e. Inquiring: Check out trainees' perceptions and assumptions.

    f. Suggesting: Ask if the trainees would like to work on the situation in the group.

    Avoid the following:

    Preaching

    Telling the trainees what to do

    Condescending remarks

    Punishing remarks

Application for Trainees After the Group Meeting

1. Have trainees make logs for the next meeting.

2. Ask trainees to study Exercise 10.5 and be prepared for the next group meeting.

EXERCISE 10.5
ASSERTIVE RIGHTS

Goal

To review the basic assertive rights and to assist the trainees in saying "no." There may be time to process some of the logs.

Time Needed—Trainee's preparation: 5 to 60 minutes for this exercise
Group work: 45 to 60 minutes

Introduction to the Exercise

After reading the basic rights, the trainees at times take these rights to the extreme. It is important to discuss this carefully. Many trainees have a difficult time learning to say "no." These exercises will help.

Training Procedures

1. Ask the trainees to turn in their logs and assign logs for the next meeting.

2. Read the Basic Assertive Rights statements.

3. Discuss the Basic Assertive Rights and ask the discussion questions from *Peer Power, Book One, Workbook*.

4. Have trainees move into groups of two each.

5. Ask one to play the persuader, who says only "yes." Ask for a trainee to recall a situation in which he/she really wanted to convince someone of something.

6. Have the other member of the dyad play the role of the refuser, who says only "no."

7. Ask the two to face each other and use appropriate tones of voice.

8. Have them change roles.

9. Circulate among the dyads and observe the interaction.

10. Discuss the following questions:

   a. Which role was easier for you? How was it easier?

   b. What did you notice about your ability to say no?

   c. Were you able to keep eye contact?

   d. What did the persuader do that made it difficult for you?

   e. In what situations or with whom do you often find yourself giving in instead of saying "no"?

   f. Do you have the right to say "no"? When? With whom? About what?

   g. How do apologizing, making excuses, and feeling guilty apply to saying "no"?

Application for Trainees After the Group Meeting

1. Have trainees continue to keep logs.

2. Ask trainees to practice saying "no."

3. Ask trainees to study Exercise 10.6 before the next group meeting.

EXERCISE 10.6
PUTTING ASSERTIVE SKILLS INTO ACTION

Goal

To have trainees practice skills learned in assertiveness and incorporate some of the skills previously learned in Module IX

Time Needed—Trainees' preparation: 10 to 20 minutes for this
exercise
Group work: 45 to 60 minutes

Introduction to the Exercise

This exercise enables trainees to practice skills of assertiveness in a safe situation. This exercise reviews earlier material
and enables the trainer to evaluate whether or not the trainees
have learned the skill.

Training Procedures

1. Collect logs, and return earlier logs. Ask if anyone would
   like to practice situations from some of the logs.

2. Have trainees divide into threes. Have each play one of
   three roles: the person being assertive, the person creating
   the problem, and an observer (use observation sheet).

3. Change roles until each trainee has played each role.

4. Circulate around the groups giving feedback.

5. Discuss the experience. How does this apply to their daily
   life?

Application for Trainees After the Group Meeting

1. Have trainees keep one more log to be turned in at the next
   meeting.

2. Study and complete Exercise 11.1 before the next group
   meeting.

3. Complete reactions to Module X.

CONFRONTATION SKILL

INTRODUCTION

In talking with or observing others, one often receives conflicting messages. As a peer helper, each trainee needs to be able to communicate to the helpee a double message and to do so in a manner that will be helpful to the helpee. The skill of pointing out and communicating about the double message is entitled confrontation, and when done properly, it enables the helper to identify the two messages without creating anger or defensive behavior on the helpee's part or the helper's.

Three general situations in which double messages (discrepancies) may occur and for which helpers may find confrontation needed are when a difference exists between:

1. What is said and what is done by the helpee

2. What the helper has been saying and what others have reported the helpee as doing

3. What the helpee says and how the helpee feels or looks

When the confrontation is used, it must be done with skill and in a manner that hopefully will be meaningful to the helpee. The five characteristics of confrontation are listed in the introductory material for Module XI in *Peer Power, Book One, Workbook*.

The number of training sessions needed will depend upon trainees and the time block for each session. All three exercises could be taught in the same session if needed. We recommend two training sessions with Exercises 11.1 and 11.2 in the first session and possibly the demonstration in preparation for Exercise 11.3, which would be in the second training session.

This module can be used in drug and alcohol intervention training, for confronting people to seek professional help, and in employer–employee, parent–child, or teacher–student relationships. It is best used with older youth and adults.

Goal

To enable trainees to learn confrontation skill and use it effectively

Time Needed—Trainees' preparation: ¾ to 1¼ hours for three sessions
Group work: 1½ to 2½ hours for three exercises

Materials

- *Peer Power, Book One, Workbook* (one for each trainee)
- Flip chart paper or whiteboard
- Pencil or pen for each trainee
- Name tag for name on shirt
- Sticky notes for trainees to utilize during training
- Snacks for trainees if budget permits
- Crayons
- Koosh balls or other things to hold in their hands
- Rewards to give to trainees at appropriate times (M&M's, etc.)
- Optional: Video equipment with previously produced video containing one or more examples of the behavior being taught

- Optional: CD to play music to bring trainees together (you may want to have a theme song or music by this time such as "Lean on Me" or other appropriate music agreed upon by the group)

Training Procedures

1. Decide the number of training sessions and the exercise to be included in each session.

2. Review the content to be covered and the suggested activities as listed in the *Peer Power, Book One, Workbook* in addition to those listed in this book.

3. Be prepared to do the demonstration as suggested or have video equipment with previously prepared recording of the behaviors to be taught.

4. If available, use the video to demonstrate skills.

5. Recognize that those who have feeling types and/or introverted types of personality will have a more difficult time with this exercise.

Evaluation Process

As trainer evaluate the process used in the teaching of the skill by the feedback obtained from the trainees and by observations of them during the times when they are asked to use the skill.

Measuring Outcomes

1. Use Exercises 11.1 and 11.2 sheets to determine how well the trainees can identify correct confrontation responses.

2. Observe and listen during role-playing in Exercise 11.3 to measure the ease with which trainees are using confrontation and the other peer helping skills.

3. Use Exercise 11.3 sheets to determine how well the trainees use the peer helping skills and how well they can identify the skills when used by others.

EXERCISE 11.1
CONDITIONS OF CONFRONTATION

Goal

To assist trainees in learning under what conditions confrontation can be helpful, including the kinds of relationships necessary between helpee and helper

Time Needed—Trainees' preparation: 15 to 30 minutes for this exercise
Group work: 30 to 60 minutes

Introduction to the Exercise

Confrontation necessitates a combination of two other skills—empathy and genuineness. This is because confrontation is done to free other individuals to be involved with the helpees while behavior changes are undertaken.

The quality of the relationship between the helpee and helper should be such that the helper can be genuine, exhibit empathy, and summarize. A helper must believe that the helpee will want to change if made aware of the double messages being communicated.

It also is important for the helper to believe that the helpee has the ability to act upon the confrontation. If the ability is lacking and confrontation occurs, the helpee could be hurt instead of helped. The trainer must help trainees understand conditions that must exist before using confrontation.

Training Procedures

1. Teach characteristics of confrontation, situations in which double messages generally occur, and conditions that must exist before confrontation is appropriate.

2. Assist trainees in overcoming their concerns related to confrontation.

3. Discuss with trainees their written material from the applications for Exercise 11.1.

4. Have trainees discuss in the group meeting their responses to Directions #4 and #5 as completed in their application for this exercise.

5. Have trainees summarize what they learned.

6. Collect Exercise 11.1 sheets and Exercise 10.9 if not collected previously.

Application for Trainees After the Group Meeting

1. If Exercise 11.1 is taught in a training session, separate from Exercises 11.2 and 11.3 and assign these two as applications to be completed before the next training session.

2. If Exercises 11.1 and 11.2 are to be taught in the same training session, move directly into Exercise 11.3.

EXERCISE 11.2
PERCEIVING CONFRONTATION SKILL

Goal

To provide written material for the trainees to study and to rate for confrontation skill

Time Needed—Trainees' preparation: 15 to 20 minutes for this exercise
Group work: 15 to 30 minutes

Introduction to the Exercise

In Exercise 11.1, trainees learned about confrontation. In Exercise 11.2, they have an opportunity to practice rating written confrontation responses to two different situations. Rating can be done as an application and discussed during the training session.

Training Procedures

1. Discuss with trainees their ratings for the confrontation responses in Exercise 10.2, *Peer Power, Book One, Workbook.*

2. Assist the trainees in learning how to rate confrontation responses.

3. Have trainees discuss their experience in rating the three situations.

4. Collect Exercise 11.2 sheets.

5. Return any exercise sheets collected in a previous training session.

Application for Trainees After the Group Meeting

If trainees have not been instructed to do so, ask them to study Exercise 11.3 and be prepared to complete it during the next training session.

EXERCISE 11.3
PRACTICE CONFRONTATION SKILL
AND RATING THE HELPER

Goal

To provide practice in confrontation skill

Time Needed—Trainees' preparation: 5 to 10 minutes for this exercise
Group work: 45 to 60 minutes

Introduction to the Exercise

This exercise is designed to provide trainees with practice in confrontation skill. They are asked to use the other peer helping skills they have learned when appropriate.

A Rating Flow Sheet is provided in *Peer Power, Book One, Workbook,* which will enable the rater to record during the role-playing. At the close of the role-playing extended dialogue, the rater can provide feedback to the helper. Often the feedback results in interchange between the rater and helper, which can provide opportunity for use of the peer helping skills. The trainer often can learn what needs to be emphasized by observing during the feedback period.

Training Procedures

1. Explain and discuss any aspects of confrontation skill that the trainees do not know. The basic concepts are presented in Module XI and the related exercises in *Peer Power, Book One, Workbook.*

2. Model the behavior before having the trainees practice. This procedure is important. Optional: Use video equipment to show the skill and as a basis for discussion.

3. Have trainees form clusters of three for practice and ask them to follow the directions in *Peer Power, Book One, Workbook,* Exercise 11.3. Review the steps within the directions to assure that the trainees understand the procedure.

4. In the initial practice exercises, have the trainees go through three to six interchanges (helper responses with emphasis on confrontation) before they stop to rate the helper.

5. Ask the rater to use the space provided in *Peer Power, Book One, Workbook* following the heading "Practice Situations."

6. Repeat the practice exercise until all trainees have played each role.

7. Upon completion of each practice, discuss the experience.

8. Repeat practice until trainees understand and can use confrontation skill.

9. Have the trainees participate in extended dialogue during role-playing in which they integrate the seven skills learned to date. Using the same triad cluster, have the helpee use real situations for an extended dialogue of at least eight

helper responses. Ask the rater in each triad to rate the helper on all peer helping skills learned by using the Flow Sheet for Rating Confrontation and other Communication Skills (in *Peer Power, Book One, Workbook*, Exercise 11.3).

10. Following practice rounds, discuss experiences the trainees had and assist them in overcoming their concerns.

11. Collect Exercise 11.3 sheets.

12. Return any exercise sheets collected in a previous training session that have not been returned.

Application for Trainees After the Group Meeting

1. Ask trainees to study the introduction to Module XII.

2. If Exercises 12.1 and 12.2 are both to be included in the next training session, ask trainees to study the seven steps to problem solving and the related dialogue and come to the next session prepared to discuss Exercises 12.1 and 12.2.

3. If only Exercise 12.1 is to be covered in the next training session, ask trainees to study it before the next session.

4. Write your reaction to Module XI. Ask two trainees to volunteer to discuss their reactions.

PROBLEM-
SOLVING SKILL

INTRODUCTION

Helping is worthwhile only if the problems causing people trouble can be solved. Therefore, for help to be effective the help that is provided needs to include a problem-solving component. Problem solving is the action behavior that brings about change. Without action, exploring and understanding the dimension of a problem are of little ultimate value.

Goal

To have trainees understand and demonstrate problem-solving strategies

Time Needed—Trainees' preparation: 1½ to 2¾ hours for these four exercises
Group work: 1¾ to 2¾ hours for these four exercises

Materials

- *Peer Power, Book One, Workbook* (one for each trainee)
- Flip chart paper or whiteboard

- Pencil or pen for each trainee
- Name tag for name on shirt
- Sticky notes for trainees to utilize during training
- Snacks for trainees if budget permits
- Crayons
- Koosh balls or other things to hold in their hands
- Rewards to give to trainees at appropriate times (M&M's, etc.)
- Optional: Video equipment with previously produced video containing one or more examples of the behavior being taught
- Optional: CD to play music to bring trainees together (you may want to have a theme song or music by this time such as "Lean on Me" or other appropriate music agreed upon by the group)
- Audio recorder for every three trainees

Tips

Effective problem solving is possible only after the helper and helpee have explored and understood all the dimensions of the problem. When this has been accomplished, the helpee is in a position to make some commitments to a behavior change. In the training of helpers the teaching of a complete problem-solving model is important if the trainees are to learn effective skills. Only after trainees have a thorough knowledge of at least one problem-solving procedure can they be flexible in how to proceed with this part of the helping process.

Each trainee, as a peer helper, can listen with ease at this point in the training to problems and concerns of others. Helping others to explore and understand is a good start in peer helping and often is all that is necessary, because a sounding board may be all the peers need. However, many times listening and understanding do not go far enough. A helpee may need to take some action in order to grow. This action behavior can take the form of problem solving. In these situations, unless trainees have each participated in the helpee's solving of problems, listening is not enough.

Many ways are available to solve problems. Having trainees use the communication skills learned is one of those ways. When listening is not enough, trainees will need some other problem-solving techniques. In the problem-solving skill module you will provide new ways for trainees to help others arrive at problem-solving action. Special emphasis will need to be made that trainees are not to solve helpees' problems for them; rather the intent is to facilitate helpees taking action.

Stress that probably not all of these skills will be used each time, but that the different techniques are useful after having done a good job of exploring and understanding and after the trainees are ready to take the final step toward behavior change. In addition, learning the problem-solving skills will benefit each trainee whenever he/she wants to change behavior and needs ways to make this change.

Module XII presents one detailed and structured model that incorporates many of the generally accepted concepts for good problem-solving behaviors. The purpose of the module is to develop a complete but simple training model that can be incorporated into an effective peer training program without going into a highly complicated and technical process.

The problem-solving model to be used includes the following seven general procedures, which are listed as the seven steps in problem solving:

Step 1. Explore the problem

Step 2. Understand the problem

Step 3. Define the problem

Step 4. Brainstorm all alternatives

Step 5. Evaluate alternatives

Step 6. Decide on the best alternative

Step 7. Implement the selected alternative

In this module each step is defined, and its purpose is explained. In addition, teaching procedures include an example of how the process operates, and in this way, one can walk the trainees through the complete module before they practice the process on their own. These procedures are outlined in *Peer Power, Book One, Workbook*, Module XII, and are to be used during the group meeting.

Exercises to be covered in each training session will depend upon time block and the practice and teaching needed by trainees. The recommendation is for a minimum of two training sessions. From the following three patterns choose the best pattern for your conditions:

Two sessions—Do Exercises 12.1 and 12.2 together and then 12.3 and 12.4.

Three sessions—Do Exercises 12.1 and 12.2 together, then 12.3 in second session, and 12.4 in third session.

Four sessions—Do one exercise in each session.

Training Procedures

1. Read through the seven steps in the problem-solving model presented in this book and in the trainee workbook for Exercise 12.1, including the definition of terms, before explaining the process to trainees. When teaching the process the trainer must understand the process fully.

2. Review the format for trainee exercises as presented in *Peer Power, Book One, Workbook*, Module XII.

3. In teaching the module, explain the entire seven steps in one session. After the module has been explained in its entirety, give examples or role-play specific procedures for practice before the model is implemented. Brainstorming, evaluating the alternatives, deciding the best alternative, and implementing the selected alternative are steps that need to be practiced with individual examples. Exploring and understanding have been practiced often in previous modules. After practicing the individual steps separately, try putting the whole process together.

4. Follow the sequence of four exercises presented for Module XII.

5. If available, use the video to demonstrate the skills.

6. Consider personality type information in helping trainees go through problem solving.

For example, trainees with dominant Sensing types will look for specifics and be good at concrete action plans. Dominant Intuitive types will be good at brainstorming and seeing the big picture. Dominant Thinking types will seek to find solutions that are based on what is fair to all. Dominant Feeling types will seek solutions that take individual issues and feelings into account. You may have to help trainees that do not have two of these letters in their preferred type to work more at these things. For example, an ENTP does not have S or F. Therefore, they would need to work on a concrete action plan and consider the impact on people.

If the trainee has Judging ("J") in their preference, they will try to rush the helpee to decide too quickly. However, it is important to move them to some direction. If the trainee has Perceiving ("P") in their preference, they will try to help the helpee look at options and not decide too quickly. This is a strength if solutions are not positive.

Evaluation Process

Determine the effectiveness of the training by how well the trainees complete the problem-solving strategies from the exploring stage through understanding to implementing the selected alternative.

Measuring Outcomes

The purpose of this module will be achieved when the trainees solve their problems by effectively using the strategies taught.

EXERCISE 12.1
PROBLEM-SOLVING PROCEDURES

Goal

To have the trainees learn the problem-solving procedures

Time Needed—Trainees' preparation: 20 to 30 minutes for this exercise
Group work: 20 to 30 minutes

Introduction to the Exercise

In Exercise 12.1 trainees are introduced to the seven steps of problem solving. *Peer Power, Book One, Workbook* has lists of what the helpee does in each step, and what the helper's procedures and skills are in problem solving. The trainer will need to review the information supplied in *Peer Power, Book One, Workbook*, Exercise 12.1.

The material is to be studied by the trainees as an application, but explanation and discussions should take place during the training session to assure understanding. The problem-solving skill is one that trainees generally want to learn. It often requires extended time, however, because their prior experience frequently has not been of using a developmental process but rather of acting with no examination of the how or why.

Training Procedures

1. Use chalkboard, flip pad, flannel board, or other means to accentuate ideas when discussing each step with trainees.

2. Identify the peer helping skills that the helper can use at each step and place these beside the steps. Help trainees understand how each skill could be used at each step.

Step	Skill(s) used
1. Exploring the problem	Empathy, attending, open-ended questioning
2. Understanding the problem	Empathy, attending, open-ended questioning, genuineness, confrontation
3. Defining the problem	Summarizing
4. Brainstorming all alternatives	Open-ended questioning
5. Evaluating alternatives	Open-ended questioning, summarizing
6. Deciding the best alternative	Empathy, attending, open-ended questioning, summarizing
7. Implementing the selected alternative	Open-ended questioning, summarizing

3. Illustrate, with samples, helpee statements and helper responses as each step is explained.

4. Encourage discussion and assist trainees in overcoming their fears.

5. Return Exercise 11.3 sheets with written comments.

Application for Trainees After the Group Meeting

1. If Exercise 12.2 is taught in the next training session instead of being taught with 12.1, ask the trainees to study the dialogue and come prepared to discuss Exercise 11.2 during the next training session.

2. If Exercises 12.2 and 12.3 are to be taught together, ask trainees to study Exercise 12.3 as well, and come prepared to complete it during the next training session.

EXERCISE 12.2
PROBLEM-SOLVING DIALOGUE

Goal

To familiarize trainees with the dialogue used in the seven steps in problem solving

Time Needed—Trainees' preparation: 30 to 45 minutes for this exercise
Group work: 15 to 30 minutes

Introduction to the Exercise

Exercise 12.2 can help trainees bring it together, use various skills, and become familiar with an overall dialogue during the helping process. If the trainees study the sample dialogue provided, they can come to the training session prepared to integrate skills learned previously.

Training Procedures

1. Review the seven steps with the trainees.

2. Proceed through the dialogue with the trainees and explain the purpose of each step and how the dialogue illustrates

the problem-solving step. Trainees have a copy of dialogue in *Peer Power, Book One, Workbook,* Exercise 12.2. Use the dialogue and explanation provided or modify it to be in keeping with your style of teaching. You might ask different trainees to play roles.

3. Assist trainees in overcoming their fears.

4. Call attention to the ease with which the dialogue moves from one step to the next.

Dialogue and Explanations for the Seven Steps

Step 1: Explore the Problem

To explore the problem means to look at the surface dimensions of the concern. This process incorporates some of the skills learned so far: attending, empathy, summarizing, open-ended questioning, and confrontation.

Sample interchange that explores the problem:

Helpee: "I don't know what job to get once I get out of school."

Helper: "You're unsure of the kind of job you want?"

Helpee: "Yeah, I think I want to get into the medical area, but I am not sure."

Helper: "You find medical careers intriguing, but you are not sure."

Helpee: "That is what I think I am working toward because I have taken nothing but science courses since I have been in high school."

Helper: "What jobs in the medical field have you considered?"

Helpee: "I have thought about becoming a doctor, but I don't think I could make it, so I guess I will be a nurse."

Exploring the problem usually takes place during the early stages of the helping relationship but can be reinitiated anytime during the process as new conditions or materials are introduced into the problem. High empathy, attending, and genuineness are the skills most often employed in this initial stage of the helping process.

Step 2: Understand the Problem

To understand the problem means to increase the helpee's awareness of how the many aspects of the concern fit together to create the issues that are causing the difficulties. Understanding usually develops when underlying feelings are brought out and dealt with. To understand necessitates involving the helper and helpee in dialogue attempting to uncover all of the conditions both internal and external that are causing the helpee difficulty. To fully understand a helpee's concern requires use of all of the skills learned so far. Empathy and attending are still the most frequently employed skills learned, but genuineness and confrontation become strong components of the understanding dimension.

Sample interchange on understanding the problem:

Helper: "You really would like to be a doctor, but it might be too hard to make it."

Helpee: "Yes, it takes so long to go to school, and I don't know whether I have the stamina to make it."

Helper: "You feel uncertain if you have the energy to make it through medical school."

Helpee: "Being a doctor is something I have always wanted to do, and my family has been planning on me going."

Helper: "I hear you saying two things. You really want to do it, and you have support, but you seem to not have confidence in yourself that you can make it."

Helpee: "Yes, self-confidence is something I hardly ever have. I convince myself that I can't do certain things, and it really hurts when I go ahead and do things."

Helper: "You put yourself down a lot. I guess I feel uncomfortable when you put yourself down, and it causes me to suggest other careers for you that you will have the confidence to do. It concerns me that you may regret it later."

Helpee: "It seems like the more I talk about my lack of self-confidence, others feel sorry for me, and they tell me I can do it. I don't need a pep talk from others."

The ability to fully understand the concern can take place only after the issues have been fully explored. When understanding occurs, helpees become aware not only of where they are but also of where they want to be. The helpee's desire to bring about personal change is an important aspect of the understanding level of awareness.

Step 3: Define the Problem

To define the problem means to articulate the issues causing the difficulty in as specific terms as possible. The more precise the terms that can be used to identify the problem the higher the probability that solutions can be found. Defining the problem includes both deficits that create the problem and the goals that are desired.

The problems (or deficits) and goals can be defined in useful terms after an adequate exploration and understanding of the problem has taken place. Without these first two dimensions, the problem-solving process becomes inappropriate because too many unknown issues, concerns, or attitudes exist that affect the problem; thus the helpee is unable to develop any solution that will work.

Step 4: Brainstorm Alternatives

The process of brainstorming is generally understood in human relations training. Brainstorming essentially means that all procedures or alternatives that could help solve a problem are introduced without criticism or comment as to their problem-solving effectiveness. An important point to teach is that both the helpee and helper have the responsibility to supply as many brainstorming ideas as possible.

The following are guidelines for brainstorming. You may want to put them on the wall and take them through a sample brainstorming technique.

Brainstorming

1. Say anything that comes to mind.

2. Don't judge your ideas or the ideas of others.

3. All ideas are accepted. Each person is encouraged to contribute ideas.

4. Invite your mind to be absolutely creative. (Don't limit your ideas.)

5. Let your thoughts come quickly. (Think of as many creative ideas as you can.)

6. Build on ideas of others. (Someone else's idea can make you think of another idea.)

7. Set a time limit and stick to it.

Sample interchange that uses brainstorming technique:

Helper: "Let's look at some ways to find answers about yourself and feel good about you. I will write ideas down and keep notes. Let's not evaluate any of the ideas. Let's just keep notes."

Helpee: "Well, I could sign up for counseling or take some of those courses on understanding yourself."

(Helper writes two ideas—"counseling" and "self-help course.")

Helper: "You could take a series of tests to see your strengths and weakness as far as ability."

(Helper writes "testing.")

Helpee: "I could ask friends what they think about me, or I could just spend time thinking about it."

(Helper writes "ask friends.")

Helper: "You could ask your family or teachers how they see your abilities."

(Helper writes "ask family or teachers.")

Helpee: "I could sign up for one of the Exploration Groups at school."

(Helper writes "Human Potential Groups.")

When teaching brainstorming, have the trainee group choose a simple problem and then practice the brainstorming technique with one member of the group. Writing all of the ideas generated by the group is helpful. In this way each trainee has the opportunity to experience how the process operates. When teaching the trainees to brainstorm, one can teach them to write each idea. Later when they have practiced the process, it will not always be necessary to write each idea. However, to write the brainstorming thoughts so they can be appraised in total upon completion of the activity usually is valuable. One of the final steps in problem solving is to reduce all of the ideas generated in brainstorming to one or two workable alternatives, and having them written facilitates the evaluation of the final choice patterns.

Step 5: Evaluate Alternatives

To evaluate alternatives means to link the values and the strengths and the weaknesses of the helpee that relate to the issue with the alternatives generated during the brainstorming activity. A helpee's values that relate to the issues exert a great deal of influence over the final decision-making process. If these influencing values are ignored in choosing a solution, the probability of a successful outcome is reduced considerably.

Since people's behavior and attitude are so strongly affected by the values they hold, linking the affected values with all possible alternatives identified is extremely important in order to arrive at an alternative that will receive full support of the helpee because the solution is compatible with his/her value system.

In teaching trainees to consider those values that will affect the alternatives chosen, having the helper list the helpee's values is important so that the values can be considered along with each of the alternatives chosen in the brainstorming activity.

Strengths—When listing the values, teach the trainees to work with the helpee in identifying strengths that can be brought to bear in solving the problem. As in the case of listing values, an important point is to have the helpee be the one to identify the values, the strengths, and later, the weakness that will influence the final alternative chosen. The helper can only suggest possible strengths and weaknesses the helpee may have but cannot establish a value system for a helpee.

Weaknesses—Along with strengths and equally important to explore are the weaknesses that will affect the final alternative chosen. When the values, strengths, and weaknesses that are brought to bear on the final solution are understood, the final decision as to which alternative has the best probability for success can be made. Without incorporating all of the three constructs, the final decision will be less likely to withstand the pressures when implementation is initiated.

With many problems the helper will recognize that the alternatives possible, the values affecting the alternatives, and the strengths and weaknesses of the helpee may be few in number and not require several lists to establish the total picture. However, in teaching the process, be sure to have the trainees write alternatives, values, strengths, and weaknesses in order to establish that they know the process and how it operates. Without this step in the training, trainees have a tendency to gloss over the process in their anxiety and their desire to arrive at a solution, but this step is very necessary in arriving at an effective solution.

Before choosing the best alternative, have the trainees identify and underline the helpee's most important value(s) that relate to the problem and the strength(s) that would most easily facilitate a successful solution to the concern.

Sample interchange that evaluates alternatives:

Helper: "Let's look at the list of suggested alternatives and then figure if any of your values are applicable to these alternatives. Then let's look at your strengths and weakness that are applicable to each alternative. We can do it by making two charts that will compare each of the qualities with which we are working."

Through working with the helpee, the helper and the helpee have identified important values held by the helpee. In the case illustrated five important values were identified—having independence, gaining an education, doing well on tests, having a family life, and having friends. These five values were used in a chart to examine whether or not each alternative would be appropriate for each value held. The "Comparison Chart of Values for Each Alternative" is shown in the workbook.

Following the completion of the "Comparison Chart of Values for Each Alternative," the helper used another chart to enable the helpee to examine strengths and weaknesses of the helpee as related to each alternative. The "Comparison Chart of Alternatives to Strengths and Weaknesses" is shown for the illustrative case.

Comparison Chart of Alternatives to Strengths and Weaknesses

Alternatives	Strengths	Weaknesses	Strongest potential character
1. Counseling	Solve things myself	Time (lack of)	Strength
2. Self-help course	Learn quickly	Time (lack of)	Weakness
3. Testing	Do well on tests	Fear of results	Strength
4. Ask family	Communicate openly	Family reaction	Strength
5. Ask friends	Leadership	Can't trust	Weakness
6. Human	Like to talk	Time (lack of)	Weakness
7. Exploration group			

Step 6: Decide on the Best Alternative

Choosing here means locating which one or two of the alternatives appear best from the brainstorming work, the developed list of values, and the identification of strengths and weaknesses of the helpee. In teaching this step of problem solving, a series of questions can be used to develop a checklist of data that will enable the helper and helpee to compare each alternative to a single set of criteria. Thus, each solution is compared to the same conditions, and the decision as to which alternative appears to be the most effective solution is more easily made.

Checklist to evaluate each alternative identified

1. Do I have all of the data available?

2. Is the alternative specific?

3. Is the alternative conceivable?

4. Is the alternative believable?

5. Does the alternative coincide with many of my values?

6. Does the alternative help me to grow as a person?

7. Is the alternative controllable?

8. Is the alternative what I want to do?

Completing the checklist will usually eliminate all but two feasible alternatives. Have the helpee circle the alternatives that are usable. Trainees need to be taught that a commitment by the helpee to act on one of the alternatives is the next necessary step to solving the helpee's problem.

Sample interchange that decides the best alternative:

Helper: "Underline the top value and best strength. There are several choices, but it looks like your best choice might be Human Potential Group and a self-help course."

Helpee: "Yes, because I enjoy learning about myself and learning in general. I am not afraid to talk about myself, and I learn quickly."

Helper: "Let me ask you some questions about your decision. Is the alternative specific? Is it clear?"

Helpee: "Yes."

Helper: "Does the alternative coincide with your values?"

Helpee: "Yes."

Helper: "Will the alternative help you grow as a person?"

Helpee: "Yes."

Helper: "Is it something that is in the realm of your control?"

Helpee: "Yes."

Helper: "Do you want to do it?"

Helpee: "Yes."

Step 7: Implement the Selected Alternative

The final step in this problem-solving model is to implement the selected alternative that (a) satisfies the most appropriate helpee values, (b) uses and implements the most important strengths, and (c) minimizes the helpee's deficiencies. This requires that the trainees be taught how to implement a plan of action using the alternative chosen.

A plan of action incorporates several necessary phases that assist in its development. Assuming that one alternative has been chosen as most appropriate and stands the best chance of effectively solving the problem, the helpee must ask and respond to several action questions:

What are my goals that need to be met in order to solve this problem?

What is the first action necessary to put the plan into operation?

What are the next activities that are necessary in the plan and in what sequence must they take place in order to reach my goal?

What obstacles are in the way of reaching the goal?

What strengths do I have to overcome the obstacles?

Who are the people who will be involved in the plan of action and how will they be involved?

What are the timelines needed for me to reach my goals?

Where do I put this plan of action into effect?

When do I take my first action?

Sample interchange that examines implementing the alternative:

Helper: "Now comes the hardest part of figuring out ways of implementing alternatives. Will the alternative help you meet your goals of understanding yourself now and feeling good about yourself?"

Helpee: "Yes."

Helper: "What steps must you take to accomplish the alternative?"

Helpee: "I can sign up for Human Potential Group with my counselor and probably go see the counselor about a self-help course."

Helper: "I really wonder what strengths you possess that will help you overcome your lack of confidence."

Helpee: "Well, I like to learn, and I stick to things once I have decided."

Helper: "Will anyone else be involved?"

Helpee: "My counselor."

Helper: "When are you going to see the counselor?"

Helpee: "This week because the Exploration Group starts soon, and I hope to take the course in the summer."

Helper: "Where do you go?"

Helpee: "Guidance Center."

Helper: "What is your first step?"

Helpee: "Talk to the counselor."

Application for Trainees After the Group Meeting

1. Have trainees study the sample dialogue again if any of the seven steps is not understood.

2. Have trainees review the purposes for each of the seven steps and the means for achieving each.

3. Have each trainee think of a situation (a problem) that is or has been real to him/her and is one that he/she is willing to practice during the next training session.

4. Ask trainees to review Exercise 12.3 in the *Peer Power, Book One, Workbook*, and be prepared to do the exercise during the next training session.

EXERCISE 12.3
PRACTICE PROBLEM-SOLVING SKILL

Goal

To provide supervised practice rounds of the seven steps in problem solving so that trainees will learn how to utilize the seven steps and related information appropriately

Time Needed—Trainees' preparation: 10 to 30 minutes for this exercise
Group work: 45 to 60 minutes

Introduction to the Exercise

The trainer will find it difficult to structure precisely this part of the training because the problem-solving aspect of helping comes toward the end of the helper–helpee relationship, and each problem takes its own particular route and has it own particular idiosyncrasies. As a result, precise, real situations and procedures cannot easily be planned for teaching purposes. The one effective way to teach this aspect is to develop a role-playing situation that will arbitrarily illustrate all seven steps in problem-solving procedures.

The trainer can best illustrate this module by dramatizing the seven steps through a role-playing situation with one or more of the trainees. In this way, each of the steps is illustrated, even though the role-playing is in reality a canned version of how the procedure works. Practice by the trainees will be the best learning condition as to the effectiveness of the training process using the model described. In the role-playing experience, the trainer will take the helper role.

Training Procedures

1. Demonstrate the seven steps through a practice situation with one or more of the trainees.

Optional: Play a video situation that will illustrate the seven steps.

2. Discuss with the trainees each of the seven steps dramatized through role-playing.

3. Have the trainees divide into clusters of two and take real problems through the seven steps of problem solving using the worksheets found in *Peer Power, Book One, Workbook,* Exercise 12.3. The helper is to complete the sheet during the role-playing.

4. Following the completion of the first practice situation using the seven steps, have the trainees come together and discuss the experiences they had. The helper from each cluster of two will be able to contribute by reviewing the notes completed on the worksheets in *Peer Power, Book One, Workbook,* Exercise 12.3.

5. Have trainees reverse roles and repeat the experience.

6. Ask the trainees to come together as a total group following the second role-playing situation and discuss the experiences they had.

7. Inform the trainees that Exercise 12.3 sheets will not be collected at this time, but an application will be given for the sheets.

Application for Trainees After the Group Meeting

1. Ask trainees to review and revise where appropriate Exercise 12.3 sheets written during the role-playing and to bring the completed sheets to the next training session.

2. Suggest to trainees that each one review the role-playing situation for the following purposes:

   a. To gain a feel for what the helper did for "you" as a trainee when you were in the helpee role.

   b. To understand your strengths when "you" as a trainee were in the helper role.

3. Ask trainees to study Exercise 12.4 and complete the exercise before the next training session.

EXERCISE 12.4
PLAN OF ACTION TO ASSIST HELPEE
IN PROBLEM SOLVING

Goal

To enable trainees to develop a plan of action containing a sequence of meaningful activities that will assist another person in problem solving

Time Needed—Trainees' preparation: 30 to 45 minutes for this exercise
Group work: 30 to 45 minutes

Introduction to the Exercise

In the training sequence a helpful procedure is to have the trainees, as they work with helpees, write a plan of action for each problem-solving situation they encounter. This plan of action should be shared with the trainer for evaluation and suggestions for alteration and improvement. In this way the trainer is able to evaluate the progress of the trainees. Also, the trainer can keep in touch with the problems with which the trainees are dealing and the progress they are making. By requiring a written plan of action, the trainer can be aware of the effectiveness of the training program.

Training Procedures

1. Discuss with the trainees the worksheets in Exercise 12.4, taking each step separately, answering questions that may occur, and helping trainees to become familiar with procedures of developing a plan of action.

2. Cluster the trainees in triads and ask them to help each other complete their worksheets. Ask them to play one of the roles listed of the sample situations. If they want to use one of their own problems, this is acceptable.

3. Move from cluster to cluster and review plans with the trainees.

4. Sign plans that are approved (may need to collect the worksheets for review and approval outside of training session).

5. Write comments on plans that need revision to help trainees learn how to develop adequate plans.

6. Collect Exercise 12.3 sheets unless Exercises 12.3 and 12.4 were taught in the same training session.

Application for Trainees After the Group Meeting

1. Require trainees after the training session and after approval of each trainee's plan of action to implement their plans during the week.

2. Ask trainees to come prepared to report progress to the group at the next training session.

3. Ask trainees to study the introduction to Unit C and Strategy Development 1 in Module XIII and think about how they might apply their peer helping skills.

4. Have trainees complete Strategy Development 1 before the next group meeting.

5. Ask the trainees to complete their reaction to this problem-solving module. Discuss their reactions.

Unit C
IMPLEMENTING
A PROGRAM

IMPLEMENTING A PROGRAM

For trainees to internalize the skills learned in the previous units, they must now put them into action. Role taking is the final area for peer helpers to integrate the skills and to internalize these skills. For the trainees to really learn, they must utilize these skills. Research has shown that peer helpers keep these skills and use them into their adult lives (Tindall, Routson, & Lewis, 2003).

Therefore, Strategy Development 1 helps the trainee to set limits and know ethical guidelines. It is very important for others to know that you spend time with this topic. Often, this strategy is a selling point for the program.

The second strategy is an important concept for the trainees to know. This has to do with them setting limits themselves and taking care of themselves. There are additional resources for this section in *Peer Power, Book Two* and *Peer Power, Book Two, Workbook.*

Strategy Development 3 is utilized in many settings because conflict is a way of life in groups. Conflict mediation will truly help your group be effective within the group itself and with others. It will help them learn skills that can be used formally and informally to solve conflict.

Strategy Development 4 assists the trainees in putting their peer helping program into action. It will help them become clear about their roles and how to organize the program. This will assist your group to truly perform well. This also sets the stage for others ways to utilize peers as seen in *Peer Power, Book Two,* and *Peer Power, Book Two, Workbook.*

MODULE **XIII**

STRATEGY DEVELOPMENT

As a trainer, you have a responsibility to assist your trainees to do the following:

Check progress of learned skills.

Help assign activities for peer helpers to apply skills.

Teach ethical considerations and referral steps.

Help peer helpers to set limits by "taking care of yourself."

Help develop ownership of program by naming it and designing a logo.

Help them pull together all of their skills to assist others in solving conflicts (conflict mediation is a common beginning skill that utilizes all the skills learned previously).

Set a foundation for advanced peer helping.

This module is designed to help you and the peer helpers achieve the previously listed seven responsibilities. The four strategy developments and related exercises are as follows:

SD1—Knowing Your Limits Through Ethical Guidelines

SD2—Taking Care of You

SD3—Conflict Resolving Skills

SD4—Putting Peer Helping into Action

Module XIII Strategy Development 175

Additional resources for this module can be found with the National Association of Peer Programs. Download the Programmatic Standards and Ethical Guidelines, http://www.peerprograms.org. You may also want to download the Rubric and evaluate your basic training. These are also both found in the book by Tindall and Black (2008).

BACCHUS Network is another resource for students in higher education to attend some of the regional and national conferences on peer programs.

STRATEGY DEVELOPMENT 1

KNOWING YOUR LIMITS THROUGH ETHICAL GUIDELINES

Goal

To help the trainees know and use ethical guidelines

Time Needed—Trainees' preparation: 1 to 1½ hours for the three exercises

Group work: 2 to 3 hours for the five exercises

Materials

- *Peer Power, Book One, Workbook* (one for each trainee)
- Code of Ethics downloaded from http://www.peerprograms. org (also shown in *Peer Power, Book One*).
- Flip chart paper or whiteboard
- Pencil or pen for each trainee
- Name tag for name on shirt
- Sticky notes for trainees to utilize during training
- Snacks for trainees if budget permits
- Crayons

- Koosh balls or other things to hold in their hands

- Rewards to give to trainees at appropriate times (M&M's, etc.)

  Optional: CD to play music to bring trainees together (you may want to have a theme song or music by this time such as "Lean on Me" or other appropriate music agreed upon by the group)

Introduction to Strategy Development 1

As the peer program professional, it is important to bring home the concept of ethical guidelines in dealing with peer helping activities. You may want to give several different examples of ethical guidelines trainees have had to follow in the past such as through the military, JROTC, work, or sports and get them to give examples.

You may want to add to the National Association of Peer Programs (NAPP) Code of Ethics. This is just a basis for ethical guidelines. You may also want to develop a local resource list for the peer helpers such as hotlines and other resources. This is a good time to bring in community agencies to present their information and explain how peer helpers can refer individuals to them.

Training Procedures

1. Review the total module and decide which exercises are to be taught when.

2. Think through the concept of Code of Ethics and Referral. This is critical for the success of the program and important in order to explain to others what you are doing.

3. Assist the peer helpers to know and use the ethical guidelines.

EXERCISE SD 1.1
CODE OF ETHICS FOR THE PEER HELPER

Goals

To have the trainees become aware of the National Association of Peer Programs Code of Ethics

To assist trainees in applying the NAPP Code of Ethics to the local program

To develop a local Code of Ethics that all sign and use

Time Needed—Trainees' preparation: 15 to 20 minutes for this exercise
Group work: 45 to 60 minutes

Introduction to the Exercise

To help set guidelines for your program, it is helpful to work with an established Code of Ethics and also to write your own. Discuss what other Codes of Ethics they know about.

Training Procedures

1. Have trainees discuss the NAPP Code of Ethics (copy is in *Peer Power, Book One, Workbook*).

2. Have each trainee develop his/her own guidelines (local peer helper's code of ethics). Discussion among members may be helpful while doing so.

3. Review the poem on trust and discuss the implications for the program.

Application for Trainees After the Group Meeting

1. Ask trainees to think about situations in their lives that affect the ethical guidelines and how important it is to follow it.

2. Ask them to look for community resources in the phone book or other sources.

EXERCISE SD 1.2
DEALING WITH ETHICAL ISSUES

Goals

To help trainees apply the Code of Ethics to situations

To help trainees translate the Code of Ethics to their own behavior

Time Needed—Trainees' preparation: 5 minutes
Group work: 30 to 60 minutes

Training Procedures

1. Cluster them in groups of two and have them identify which ethical statement was violated in each of the 10 situations described. Have them add two more situations.

2. Discuss with the total group what each cluster has discovered.

3. An alternative training procedure is to assign only one example to each cluster and then have them share the ethical guideline that was violated and how the program handles the situation.

4. Lead a discussion of how to relate this to their own behavior.

Application for Trainees After the Group Meeting

1. Ask the trainees to think about ethical situations in their interactions with others.

2. Ask the trainees to look in the phone book or other local referral sources and bring at least one to the next training.

EXERCISE SD 1.3
KNOWING YOUR OWN LIMITS

Goals

To assist trainees in knowing local referral sources

To provide practice in how to refer others to sources

Time Needed—Trainees' preparation: 30 minutes
Group work: 45 minutes

Training Procedures

1. Ask trainees to share the local resources they have found, put them on a list, and ask someone in the group to make a list and give a copy to everyone.

2. As the peer program professional, bring in a list of local referrals. You may want a mental health worker or local resources expert to help with this exercise.

3. Look at the guidelines for referral. Have the trainees work in twos to develop practice in referral. Ask them to come up with three situations.

   a. Refer someone that needs prenatal care.

   b. Refer someone that needs counseling.

   c. Refer someone that needs to get help because of suicidal thoughts.

Application for Trainees After the Group Meeting

1. Continue to ask trainees to identify local referral sources.

2. Ask the trainees to think about a code of conduct that they may want to add to the ethical guidelines. In some cases, it is the same thing. However, with youth, they may need to think about their own code of conduct.

EXERCISE SD 1.4
CODE OF CONDUCT

Goals

To enable each trainee to develop individually his/her own guidelines called the Code of Conduct

Time Needed—Trainees' preparation: none
Group work: 30 minutes

Training Procedures

1. Lead a discussion on role modeling. Ask them about such things as leading a healthy lifestyle and what that means (do not expect the peer helpers to be perfect).

2. Share state laws that will guide their behavior.

3. Share local regulations of the school, university, or workplace that need to be understood by the peer helpers.

4. Discuss their own values and whether or not those values conflict with what you are doing as a peer helper.

5. Make sure that your program has developed answers to the Sample Guidelines for Code of Conduct.

Application for Trainees After the Group Meeting

1. Ask the trainees to think about their commitment to healthy role modeling.

2. Get them to think about how to network with others who are serving as peer helpers.

EXERCISE SD 1.5
NETWORKING

Goal

To help trainees think about a plan for networking

Time Needed—Trainees' preparation: 5 minutes
Group work: 30 minutes

Training Procedure

1. Set up a time and place to meet with your training group after the basic training is completed.

2. Discuss how to network with other peer helpers from other organizations.

Application for Trainees After the Group Meeting

1. Ask trainees to write reflections on Strategy Development 1.

2. Have trainees read through "Taking Care of You" in Strategy Development 2.

STRATEGY DEVELOPMENT 2

TAKING CARE OF YOU

Goal

To help trainees learn how to take care of themselves

Time Needed—Trainees' preparation: 50 minutes for the three exercises

Group work: 1 to 2 hours for the five exercises

Materials

- *Peer Power, Book One, Workbook* (one for each trainee)
- Code of Ethics downloaded from http://www.peerprograms. org (also shown in *Peer Power, Book One, Workbook*).
- Flip chart paper or whiteboard
- Pencil or pen for each trainee
- Name tag for name on shirt
- Sticky notes for trainees to utilize during training
- Snacks for trainees if budget permits
- Crayons
- Koosh balls or other things to hold in their hands
- Rewards to give to trainees at appropriate times (M&M's, etc.)

- Optional: CD to play music to bring trainees together (you may want to have a theme song or music by this time such as "Lean on Me" or other appropriate music agreed upon by the group)

Introduction to Strategy Development 2

It is important to help the trainees to develop their own support systems and also to develop a way to take care of themselves. Peer helpers naturally try to help others and get very stressed because of this. In order to help them learn helping limits, this strategy is important to know before they start their activities. Other skills are developed in *Peer Power, Book Two*.

Training Procedures

1. Assist them in identifying their own support system and learning how to access that system.

2. Help the trainees identify their own stressors and healthy ways to manage the stress.

3. Help the trainees learn how their own personality type impacts their stressors and how to manage their stress.

Evaluation Process

Determine the effectiveness of the training by how well the trainees are able to complete the exercises and apply them to their daily lives.

Measuring Outcomes

The purpose of this module will be achieved when the trainees can know and use "taking care of you" skills in their peer helping activities.

EXERCISE SD 2.1
TAKING CARE OF YOURSELF

Goal

To help trainees learn about their support system and how to bring balance into their lives

Time Needed—Trainees' preparation: 15 minutes
Group work: 30 minutes

Introduction to the Exercise

Peer helpers, because they are caring people, often overextend themselves and do not know their own limits. They are often codependent individuals who need to learn ways to take care of themselves.

Training Procedures

1. Ask trainees to list the needs they have that others can meet.
2. Ask them to make a list of people they want to have around them.
3. Ask them to fill out the chart in the workbook.
4. Have them discuss what they have learned.
5. Have them discuss what they need for balance in their lives.
6. Have each trainee identify some goals that will help in taking care of self.

   Note: Some trainees may discover they have needs but do not know how to satisfy those needs. Therefore, you as the professional must help them set goals to identify realistic means of satisfying needs.

Application for Trainees After the Group Meeting

1. Have them think and practice balance in their lives.
2. Have trainees study Exercise SD 2.2 and come to the next group meeting prepared to discuss it.

EXERCISE SD 2.2
MANAGEMENT OF STRESS

Goals

To help trainees learn their stressors

To help trainees learn their stress signals

To help trainees use tools to manage stress

Time Needed—Trainees' preparation: 10 minutes
Group work: 40 minutes

Introduction to the Exercise

Peer helpers need to be role models to others. They also need to be able to assist others with stress management. This exercise will assist them to help others.

Training Procedures

1. Ask the trainees to identify stressors prior to the training session. Ask them to be specific (e.g., I feel stressed when someone yells at me. I feel stressed in traffic.).

2. Ask the trainees to identify signals that let them know they are under stress.

3. Ask the trainees to share healthy ways that they manage stress.

4. You may want to add additional ways of managing stress.

5. As a trainer, always share your own stressors signals and how you manage stress on a daily basis.

6. Help them come up with a plan of action for managing stress.

Application for Trainees After the Group Meeting

1. Have them practice stress management.

2. Have trainees study Exercise SD 2.3 and come prepared to discuss whether or not this applies to them.

EXERCISE SD 2.3
PERSONALITY TYPE AND STRESS

Goals

To help trainees apply information learned in Module II

To help trainees to decide whether this information fits them

Time Needed—Trainees' preparation: 20 minutes
             Group work: 40 minutes

Introduction to the Exercise

Peer helpers need to be able to apply information from Module II and understand how it relates to stress.

Training Procedures

1. Review Module II and bring the "best fit" type to this section.

2. Ask the trainees to review the different types.

3. Lead a discussion about possible sources of stress and see if they agree. Are there additional ideas? Place the ideas in the notes section.

4. Ask them to see if they agree with you and each other about ways to cope with stress.

5. Lead a discussion about stress and type, and how different types have different stressors.

Application for Trainees After the Group Meeting

1. Have them think about others they know well and see if the type information applies to these others.

2. Complete the reflection on this strategy and discuss with the total group how this applies to their daily lives.

3. Read the introduction to Strategy Development 3.

STRATEGY DEVELOPMENT **3**

ASSISTING OTHERS THROUGH CONFLICT MEDIATION

Effective management of a conflict is an important and necessary tool for survival in a fast-paced, complex society. Moreover, people's development in solving conflicts, eliminating strife, and facing and making decisions—at an early age as well as through the life span—has become important. The age that seems to have the most conflict is late preadolescence and early teens. Young people tend to clash with parents, teachers, and peers. Fighting is often used as a means for resolving conflicts. The workplace also is a source of conflict. Typically, conflict that is unresolved leads to stress, sometimes mental health issues, and ultimately quitting the job or getting fired.

An effective system for managing conflicts is necessary for development; therefore, greater efforts should be focused toward increasing psychological growth and enhancing cognitive development.

Conflict, like it or not, is inevitable as long as humans relate to one another—live together, work together, associate in groups and organizations, and attend school together. While very few people go out looking for a conflict, conflict seems to find us anyway. Our differing values, opinions, and perceptions set us up for seemingly endless possibilities to have misunderstandings or differences with others. Even if we try, we can't avoid conflict.

Our inability to cope with conflict effectively causes companies to spend millions to teach conflict-resolution skills. In trying to teach conflict mediation, it is important to understand differences in personality type. At times, simply knowing type can lead to a heightened awareness that affords those in conflict better coping skills and possible alternatives during and after the altercation. People want to lead more productive, peaceful lives with family, friends, and coworkers.

Ideas presented in this module have proven to be useful in avoiding many potential conflicts and will enhance management of conflicts encountered in a confident and forceful manner. Conflict management involves emphasizing critical thinking as it requires a person to analyze values and information and apply them to specific situations.

Goals

To help trainees explore how they handle conflict personally

To help trainees identify positive ways to change some of their thinking about conflict

To train trainees in steps involved in conflict mediation

To help trainees practice conflict mediation

To help trainees apply personality type information to resolving conflict

Application for Trainees After the Group Meeting

Ongoing throughout the mediation process

Time Needed—Trainees' preparation: 35 minutes to 1½ hours for the six exercises
Group work: 3½ to 5½ hours for the six exercises

Materials

- *Peer Power, Book One, Workbook* (one for each trainee)
- Flip chart paper or whiteboard

- Pencil or pen for each trainee
- Name tag for name on shirt
- Sticky notes for trainees to utilize during training
- Snacks for trainees if budget permits
- Crayons
- Koosh balls or other things to hold in their hands
- Rewards to give to trainees at appropriate times (M&M's, etc.)
- Optional: CD to play music to bring trainees together (you may want to have a theme song or music by this time such as "Lean on Me" or other appropriate music agreed upon by the group)

Training Procedures

1. Read through the steps for conflict mediation and think of appropriate situations for trainees to practice.

2. Use the material in Exercise SD 3.6 as practice. It can be used several times for practice.

3. Once the trainees have learned conflict mediation, provide them with an opportunity to do this in a formal way by conducting formal mediations. They may also use it informally with the other skills when they observe others in conflict.

4. Use the personality type material in Module II to assist in work with trainees. In the conflict literature, the general consensus is that both personality and situational variables significantly influence the approach people use to handle conflict.

5. Recognize and help trainees understand that, in general, Thinking (T) types are more likely than Feeling (F) types to enter into a conflict. Introvert (I) Types are more likely to avoid dealing with conflict.

6. Use, if available, video equipment to help demonstrate skills.

Evaluation Process

Determine the effectiveness of the training by how well trainees are able to utilize effectively their communication skills, to follow-through steps identified in mediation, and to help others resolve conflicts.

Measuring Outcomes

The goals of Strategy Development 3 are reached when the trainees are able to effectively problem-solve and effectively mediate their own issues.

The goals of this module are reached when the trainees are able to help others resolve conflict.

EXERCISE SD 3.1
HOW I HANDLE CONFLICT

Goal

To have trainees identify how they currently handle conflict

Time Needed—Trainees' preparation: 15 to 20 minutes with daily activities for this exercise
Group work: 30 to 45 minutes

Introduction to the Exercise

Conflict seems to be a way of life; however, it takes both a psychological and physical toll on people. People often become depressed and anxious with conflict at work or at home. This leads to high blood pressure, increased heart attacks, and abuse.

The following exercise will help people to identify how conflict affects them.

Training Procedures

1. Lead a discussion about some of the situations that trainees listed in their workbooks and write them on the whiteboard.

2. Ask trainees to discuss those conflicts avoided. List answers on the whiteboard.

3. Ask trainees to discuss times in which they observed conflict and write them on the whiteboard.

4. Ask trainees to identify how the conflict affected them physically. Examples would be that their stomach hurts, verbally they spoke at a different rate, their heart rate changed, and they became very tense.

5. Ask trainees to identify how the conflict affected them psychologically. Examples would be that they became afraid, withdrawn, aggressive, mad, or disturbed in other ways.

6. Ask them to identify some of the results of the above conflicts and write them on the whiteboard.

7. Ask them to identify how comfortable they were about the conflict.

Application for Trainees After the Group Meeting

1. Ask trainees to keep a notebook concerning conflicts that they observe or in which they are involved, including how they reacted physically and what the outcome was.

2. Ask trainees to review Exercise SD 3.2 before the next group meeting.

EXERCISE SD 3.2
IMAGINING SELF IN CONFLICT

Goal

To help trainees learn relaxation techniques and to use their imagination in reference to conflicts

Time Needed—Trainees' preparation: 5 to 10 minutes plus
daily activities for this exercise
Group work: 30 to 45 minutes

Introduction to the Exercise

Imagery is a strategy to assist the trainees to feel internally that they can resolve conflict.

Training Procedures

1. Write the words *relaxation* and *imagery* on the whiteboard. You might demonstrate to trainees the difference between tension and relaxation by asking them to notice how it feels to tense their whole body and then relax their whole body. Explain to them that this is an imagery exercise and let the trainees know that imagery and relaxation will help them prevent conflicts.

2. Explain to the trainees that imagery is used to help people improve themselves in a variety of ways, such as pain management, reducing stress, improving ability to play various sports, and losing weight by thinking thin. Tell trainees that what we often practice in our mind often becomes very real in the world; therefore, we need to practice imagery so as to help us achieve our goals and values.

3. Discuss the notion that relaxation and imagery go together. Tell trainees that once people are relaxed they can introduce a positive idea to themselves more easily.

4. Ask trainees to put themselves in a very comfortable position, either lying down or leaning against the wall. You might even invite them to bring tape recorders to this particular training. Play some relaxing background music. Make sure that your voice is very slow and soft. You might practice this beforehand to ensure a soothing voice. The following is a script that might be very effective.

Please close your eyes and take a very deep breath. Remember to breathe very deeply and slowly. To help you begin this relaxation I am going to have you tense and relax some of your muscle groups. If your mind begins to wander a little just bring your mind back to my voice. So let's start with your muscles in your right hand. Make a fist. Make it very tight as I count to five and as I say the word *relax*, just relax your arm and fist. So let's start.

One, two, three, four, five. Hold it tight. (Pause.) Now relax. Now take a deep breath. Keep your eyes closed. I want you to notice the difference between the tense feelings that you just felt and the nice warm feelings of relaxation. You might notice warmth and tingling as your arm begins to relax. So let's just let go. Let your arm feel heavy and warm. You can relax a little bit more. Now relax it completely. Your arm is heavy, and your muscles are loose, and your arm is completely relaxed. Now let's relax the muscles in your left hand and arm. Make a fist and I will count to five. One, two, three, four, five. That's it. Now relax and let your arm go. Again, notice the difference between the tense feelings and the relaxed feelings, and notice the tingling and warm feelings in your arms. Just let your arm relax and let it go loose. Now let's relax your arm completely. Let's go back to your breathing. You are relaxing more and more all of the time and just breathing easily and deeply.

Now begin to relax your face. You might raise your eyebrows higher and as I count to five hold it. One, two, three, four, five. Now let your forehead smooth out. Feel your forehead getting relaxed.

The next thing you may want to work on is your eyes. Just close your eyes, tighter and tighter, as I count to five. One, two, three, four, five. Imagine your eyelids getting more and more heavy.

Feel your muscles and clench your teeth tighter and tighter as I count to five. One, two, three, four, five. Hold it tight, feel the tension and then go limp. Go ahead and let it relax. Now you are breathing deeply and freely, easily and slowly.

Now work your shoulders. Lift your shoulders higher and higher as I count to five. One, two, three, four, five. Hold your shoulders tight, and now relax.

The next area to work on is your stomach. Draw your stomach in as I count to five. One, two, three, four, five. Hold it tight. That's right. Now relax. You're breathing deeply and easily, freely and slowly. Relaxing more and more each time you breathe. Your whole body is feeling heavy and relaxed. If you feel good, you are calm and relaxed.

Now you can tense the rest of your body, tense your hips, legs, and feet as I count to five. One, two, three, four, five. Hold the muscles tight. Now let your right leg relax. Just relax your right leg. Imagine all the tension flowing out your right leg and into the air. Imagine your left leg relaxing. It is getting very limp and loose. Now your body is relaxed and calm. As you practice this you will begin to teach yourself to relax more and more each time *you practice. Your body will feel calm and good. Now just imagine yourself becoming more and more relaxed. As you are practicing this relaxation, I want you to picture yourself feeling very relaxed and at peace with yourself.*

Now I would like for you to imagine yourself if you would, in a situation where there is conflict. Picture in your mind the conflict situation. Maybe someone disagreeing with you or criticizing you. See yourself as calm, strong, and relaxed. The anger is bouncing off of you and away. As the person becomes more angry, you become calmer. Just imagine yourself feeling very calm, and imagine yourself talking very peacefully.

At this point, I would like for you to envision yourself solving conflicts peacefully everyday. I would like for you to open your eyes and feel refreshed and relaxed. Five, four, three, two, one. Just open your eyes and feel refreshed.

5. Ask each trainee to draw a picture of him/herself solving a conflict.

6. Ask the trainee to write how it felt to resolve the conflict.

Application for Trainees After the Group Meeting

1. Ask each trainee to practice everyday this week before going to sleep by using the imagery exercise with a recording if they made one.

2. After a couple of days of practice, ask them to recall a conflict situation and try to utilize the relaxation and imagery work to solve it.

3. Ask them to complete Exercise SD 3.3 before the next group meeting.

EXERCISE SD 3.3
CHANGING CONFLICT THOUGHTS
INTO PEACEFUL THOUGHTS

Goal

To discuss differences in the impact on behavior between thinking about conflict versus thinking about peace

Time Needed—Trainees' preparation: 20 to 30 minutes for this exercise

Group work: 20 to 30 minutes

Training Procedures

1. Lead a discussion about different ways to solve problems.

2. Ask trainees to identify the messages they give themselves when in conflict and when at peace.

3. Have them discuss what they learned.

4. Ask them to develop autogenetic phrases to use when they are in conflict or when acting as a conflict mediator. Autogenetic phrases are self-generated statements that help people think and feel differently.

Examples:

"I feel calm."

"I can solve this in peace."

"I am good at solving problems through negotiation."

Application for Trainees After the Group Meeting

1. Ask trainees to record during this next week those times when they experience solving problems peacefully. They can use the questions in Direction #3 of their *Peer Power, Book One, Workbook*, as an outline for keeping the record.

2. Ask trainees to review Exercise SD 2.4 and complete as much of it as they can before the next group meeting.

EXERCISE SD 3.4
THE FOUR D's

Goal

To help trainees learn ways to stop conflict

Time Needed—Trainees' preparation: 5 to 10 minutes for this exercise

Group work: 30 to 45 minutes

Introduction to the Exercise

It is helpful to have trainees learn a quick method of dealing with conflict. This is helpful for younger youth.

Training Procedures

1. Ask them to review the four Ds listed in *Peer Power, Book One, Workbook.*

2. Have trainees give examples of each step.

3. Practice the four-step conflict stoppers.

4. Hold a discussion among trainees on ways they can avoid conflict.

Application for Trainees After the Group Meeting

1. Ask trainees to write their responses to each of the four cases provided in *Peer Power, Book One, Workbook*, Exercise SD 3.4, and bring these to the next meeting.

2. Ask them to review Exercise SD 3.5 before the next group meeting.

3. Ask trainees to use the four Ds in their everyday life and share their experiences in a group meeting.

EXERCISE SD 3.5
USING PERSONALITY TYPE TO COPE
WITH CONFLICT

Goal

To help trainees learn how different personality types handle conflict

Time Needed—Trainees' preparation: 0 to 5 minutes for this exercise
Group work: 45 to 60 minutes

Introduction to the Exercise

Different personality types feel differently about conflict and handling conflict. In any conflict mediation strategy learning how personality type plays a part is important. Few people actually go out looking for conflict. However, because of different values, cultures, and opinions, people inevitably find themselves in conflict. Therefore, learning how different personality types approach conflict is crucial.

Training Procedures

1. Cluster the trainees into two groups representing Thinking (T) type and Feeling (F) type. Keep in mind that this is how we make decisions.

   a. Ask them to respond to the questions in *Peer Power, Book One, Workbook.*

   b. Have them place answers on newsprint.

   c. After about 10 minutes, ask each group to share their answers.

   d. Point out how different types view conflict. You will find that Thinkers view conflict as a process that leads to a solution. Feelers view conflict as stressful and upsetting. Remember Feelers like harmony.

2. Have trainees to recluster into two groups—Extroverts and Introverts.

   a. Have them respond to the questions in *Peer Power, Book One, Workbook,* and place the answers on newsprint.

   b. Have them share their responses.

   c. Point out that Extroverts try to talk their way out of conflict and Introverts try to avoid conflict.

3. Recluster into Intuitive (N) types and Sensing (S) types.

   a. Show a slide or picture for one minute. Take it away.

   b. Ask each group to reproduce what they saw.

   c. You will find that Sensing types will try to duplicate the picture. Intuitives will be creative and make changes.

It is obvious that Sensing types and Intuitive types will view issues differently in conflict. How would these differences affect conflict?

4. Have the group discuss how each preference deals with conflict.

5. Ask trainees to review the suggestions for each preference and discuss whether they agree with it.

6. Lead a discussion about how knowing types is important when they are doing conflict mediation and how they are personally involved in conflict.

7. Collect the applications from Exercise SD 3.4.

Application for Trainees After the Group Meeting

1. Ask trainees to review Exercise SD 3.6.

2. Ask them to come prepared to follow through on the directions for Exercise SD 3.6.

EXERCISE SD 3.6
HELPING OTHERS THROUGH PEER MEDIATION

Goal

To help trainees role-play the specific steps in the mediation process

Time Needed—Trainees' preparation: 15 to 20 minutes for this exercise
Group work: 45 to 90 minutes (may need to be done over two group meetings)

Introduction to the Exercise

This particular exercise will help trainees learn specific steps involved in mediation. Everyone will need to do a mediation role-play successfully. These steps and this particular exercise can be utilized over and over again in follow-up training.

Training Procedures

1. Review the steps in formal mediation program. You may have set up your own procedures in your location.

2. Ask the trainees to review the steps involved in the mediation process. At this point, you may personally want to model it (i.e., demonstrate each step). At this time, you might want to put specific points on the chalkboard or around the room when you introduce yourself and make your opening statement (you may want to explain to those in conflict that you are glad that they are willing to participate and that the mediator's role is to act as a neutral party, not as a judge, fact finder, or decision maker). If available, use the video equipment to demonstrate the skills.

3. Ask trainees to recall that the emphasis of the mediation is to focus on the future and not on the past. You then may want to model how to review the guidelines and model as they are listening. Help them recognize that a contract (sample is supplied in workbook) will be signed by those in mediation as well as by the peer mediators.

4. Ask trainees to put the conflict issues in type dynamics if it fits. If so, pinpoint to a letter preference and why it might cause conflict.

5. Ask trainees to divide into groups of five. In each group two of them will be the people in conflict, two people will be the mediators, and the other will be the observer. Ask the observer to use the observer form.

6. Have the two people identify a conflict and practice the conflict while two people serve as mediators. The mediators are to go through the steps.

7. Ask the observer to give feedback to the two mediators in terms of the steps that they went through and what skills they used.

   Note: At this point your responsibility is to make sure that all trainees can use the skills effectively.

8. Return Exercise SD 3.4 with your written comments.

Application for Trainees After Group Meeting

1. Ask them to read Strategy Development 4.

2. Have them be conflict mediators, fill out their contracts, and come to the next group meeting to share experiences.

3. Ask them to complete the notes section and reactions to this Strategy Development.

STRATEGY DEVELOPMENT **4**

PUTTING PEER
HELPING INTO ACTION

When the trainees have finished the basic training, the question the trainer must answer is, "Which trainees are skillful enough to participate actively in peer helping?" The answer is not easy. For those who are ready, opportunities for doing so must be made available and supervision, support, and consultation must also be available. For those who are not skillful enough, additional assistance will be needed to assure their continued growth.

Answering the question as to which trainees are skillful enough requires objective information and professional experience. The answer to the question by some trainees may be different than the answer by the trainer. Certainly the trainer wants as much reliable information as possible before supplying the answer. The exercise sheets collected, reviewed, and commented upon in writing throughout the training program become vital. The interactions observed during training sessions have enabled the trainer to work with trainees during training sessions and in some instances outside of training sessions on an individual or small group basis. What the trainer gained during these times becomes background information for answering the question. Think through when and how trainees will be informed as to whether or not they are encouraged to become active as peer helpers.

As your peer helping group begins to plan activities, know that they will need additional training from *Peer Power, Book Two*. For example, if they are going to conduct tutoring, then train them in that module. If they are going to work with groups, train them in that module.

Early in the training program, a pretest was administered. The same items can be administered again as a post-test. The results from the post-test can be important; however, remember that the trainees have had the post-test throughout the training program, and the results may not be reliable as the base for answering the question.

If trainees are encouraged to participate as peer helpers, then plans will need to be made to facilitate their participation. Exercises SD 4.2 through SD 4.6 can assist.

Goal

To get trainees ready to implement peer helping skills by helping others

Time Needed—Trainees' preparation: 3 to 4 hours for the six exercises
Group work: 3 to 4 hours for the six exercises

Materials

- *Peer Power, Book One, Workbook* (one for each trainee)
- Flip chart paper or whiteboard
- Pencil or pen for each trainee
- Name tag for name on shirt
- Sticky notes for trainees to utilize during training
- Snacks for trainees if budget permits
- Crayons
- Koosh balls or other things to hold in their hands
- Rewards to give to trainees at appropriate times (M&M's, etc.)

- Optional: CD to play music to bring trainees together (you may want to have a theme song or music by this time such as "Lean on Me" or other appropriate music agreed upon by the group)

T-shirts or pins with the logo of your peer helping group will be given to the peer helpers at the completion of this module. Certificates of completion or credit may also be given at the conclusion along with some kind of celebration.

Introduction to Strategy Development 4

Now that the trainees are ready to take on helping in a variety of roles, it is important to create a system that will allow for support, continued training, and supervision as they begin to implement their program. The skills they have learned in basic training will enable them to perform many helping roles such as listening, mentoring, supporting, and mediation. As they identify specific activities they would like to deliver, give them additional training from *Peer Power, Book Two*.

Training Procedures

1. Have the materials/forms ready to be implemented for the program.

2. Have a plan for those trainees that you feel need additional training.

3. Be prepared to have a formal completion of the basic training through some form of recognition, celebration, and publicity.

Evaluation Process

The progress of the Peer Helping Training Program can be determined by the skills learned by the trainees and the number of them who will become actively involved in peer helping.

Measuring Outcomes

1. Count the number of trainees who become peer helpers.

2. Watch the involvement of trainees in activities where peer helping skills can be beneficial.

3. Watch progress of trainees in various groups, organizations, and activities.

4. Determine how many trainees follow through with completing Peer Helping Feedback Flow Sheets and seeking supervision and/or consultation.

5. Set up an evaluation to determine impact on the target population (those receiving help from the peer helper). Refer to the Peer Program books for sample forms for evaluation of the target population as well as the Peer Helpers.

Evaluation Process

Determine the effectiveness of the training by how well the trainees are able to complete the exercises and apply them to their helping roles and their daily lives.

EXERCISE SD 4.1
POSTTEST COMMUNICATIONS EXERCISE

Goal

To have trainees take the posttest as one means of determining readiness to participate actively in peer helping

Time Needed—Trainees' preparation: 15 to 20 minutes for this exercise
Group work: no time required

Introduction to the Exercise

The posttest items are the same as those of the pretest used in Exercise 1.1. After the posttest is administered and scored, the trainer can compare the results both for the group as a whole and for each trainee.

Training Procedures

Alternate procedure: Have the first group meeting to consist of a discussion of SD 4.1.

1. Have trainees take the posttest, Exercise SD 4.1, in *Peer Power, Book One, Workbook*.

2. Collect posttest and score it.

3. Compare results of pretest with those of posttest. This may need to be done between group meetings. If so, collect SD 4.1 sheets.

4. Review all information available to the trainer regarding each trainee.

5. Decide whether or not each trainee is to be encouraged to participate actively in peer helping.

6. Discuss with each trainee whether or not active participation in peer helping should be encouraged at this time and what alternatives exist for that individual. They may need additional training!

Application for Trainees After the Group Meeting

1. Ask trainees to review and complete Exercise SD 4.2 before the next training session.

2. Ask trainees to review Exercise SD 4.3 before the next training session.

EXERCISE SD 4.2
ORGANIZING FOR PEER HELPING

Goal

To assist trainees who will activity participate in peer helping to initiate an active role in formulating an organizational structure

Time Needed—Trainees' preparation: 30 to 45 minutes for this exercise
Group work: 30 to 45 minutes

Introduction to the Exercise

Exercise SD 4.2 is a means of helping trainees get started as peer helpers. The process includes having trainees examine and record their goals and plans of action and do a self-analysis. Criteria are suggested for checking goals. The trainees need application time for preparing Exercise SD 4.2 sheets. They generally can benefit both from interaction with one another during a training session (Exercise SD 1.2) and from talking individually with the trainer.

Training Procedures

1. Discuss with trainees selected to be peer helpers the process outlined in Exercise SD 4.2 and help them overcome their fears.

2. Cluster trainees in triads and ask them to assist one another in reviewing and completing Exercise SD 4.2 sheets.

3. Move among triads and assist where needed.

4. Discuss where trainees can apply their peer helping skills and develop a plan of action for supervision and consultation for the peer helpers.

5. Review Exercise SD 4.3 with trainees.

6. Collect Exercise SD 4.2 sheets.

7. Return any exercise sheets previously collected.

Application for Trainees After the Group Meeting

1. Ask trainees to follow the discussed plan for supervision and consultation as they actively participate as peer helpers.

2. Ask trainees to complete Exercise SD 4.3.

EXERCISE SD 4.3
IMPLEMENTING MY PEER HELPER PLAN

Goals

To have each trainee implement his/her own plan for helping

To have trainees help one another to identify strengths and potentials for improving plans

Time Needed—Trainees' preparation: 15 to 60 minutes for this exercise
Group meeting: 30 to 45 minutes

Introduction to the Exercise

To help trainees learn planning skills, it is important to have them claim ownership of the goal.

Training Procedures

1. Have trainees cluster into triads and discuss their experiences as they implemented their plans.

2. Have trainees be peer helpers to one another in terms of helping each other identify strengths of the plan and means for improving it if implemented again.

3. Have the group as a whole discuss what they learned from the experience and the implications for the future.

4. Collect Exercise SD 4.3 sheets.

Application for Trainees After the Group Meeting

Ask each trainee to review Exercise SD 4.4 and to come to the next group meeting prepared to identify a peer helper role for him/herself.

EXERCISE SD 4.4
WHAT IS YOUR ROLE?

Goal

To help trainees identify roles that they will have in the peer helping program

Time Needed—Trainees' preparation: 5 minutes for this exercise
Group work: 30 to 45 minutes

Introduction to the Exercise

Once people have learned some of the basic skills, they can apply these in a meaningful manner to help others. The research is clear that for people to feel empowered, they have to apply their skills. It is not enough just to learn the skills. They must work together. The "amount of retention" of skills is at 95% if trainees have a chance to teach or help others. The research also is clear that youth gain in moral development and character development if they have an opportunity to help others. Youth between the ages of 12 to 18 will have developed 10 to 15 assets after they have served in helping roles.

For peers to truly understand the significance of what they have done and to be able to enhance their abilities, they must have the opportunity to interact with you, the professional.

Ask the trainees to look at the list in Exercise SD 4.4 and check whether or not any of the examples provided fit their roles. If additional areas for them to use are needed, please add.

Have the trainees work with you the trainer to help them set up goals for the future. Ask them to each practice situations in which they will be involved as a peer helper. Regroup trainees into triads with one as the peer helper, one as the helpee, and one as the observer. You as the trainer may want to role-play one of the situations.

Example: Practice welcoming a new member to the group (school, business, organization). Utilize good attending, genuineness, empathy, and open-ended questions.

Help trainees set goals for their future roles. At this point, you as the professional will know the skills of the peer helper; therefore, you will need to select peer helpers you feel would be good at these roles. You need to help each peer helper find a role that he/she can perform in helping others.

Return Exercise SD 4.3 sheets with your written comments.

EXERCISE SD 4.5
LOGO AND NAME FOR HELPERS

Goal

To assist peer helpers in developing some ownership of their own name and logo

Time Needed—Trainees' preparation: 15 to 20 minutes for this exercise
Group work: 45 to 60 minutes

Training Procedures

1. Have trainees brainstorm ideas for a name of their peer helping group. Use questions provided in *Peer Power, Book One, Workbook*, in Direction #1.

2. Have trainees follow Direction #2 in their *Peer Power, Book One, Workbook*.

3. Have trainees follow Directions #3, #4, #5, and #6.

4. If a name and logo has been established, then give them a pin or shirt or other ways to identify they are now a helper.

5. Give them a certificate of completion and make a formal activity through press announcement, celebration, or other similar events.

Application for Trainees After the Group Meeting

Have trainees study Exercise SD 4.6 and be prepared to discuss it and follow the directions when the group next meets.

EXERCISE SD 4.6
PEER HELPER FEEDBACK FLOW SHEET

Goal

To provide a means of self-evaluation for each peer helper and communication between peer helper and trainer (or supervisor)

Time Needed—Trainees' preparation: 30 to 60 minutes for this exercise
Group work: no time required

Introduction to the Exercise

Peer Helper Feedback Flow Sheets will enable peer helpers to do self-analysis; hopefully, doing so will produce additional growth. Their supervisors can use the flow sheets to make comments to assist the peer helpers and when reviewed periodically to provide a means of determining progress and direction. Flow sheets also can provide a starting point when consultation is necessary. Flow sheets can be a way to conduct summative evaluation of the activities your peer helpers conduct.

Training Procedures and Application for Trainees

1. Ask peer helpers to complete a Peer Helper Feedback Flow Sheet after each peer helping contact.

2. Review flow sheet with the peer helpers, and, in a supervisory/consultative role, assist in their growth and development.

3. Ask peer helpers to respond to the notes section for reflection.

REFERENCES

Bandura, A. (1995). *Self Efficacy in Changing Society.* Cambridge: Cambridge Press.

Bandura, A. (Ed.). (2006). *Psychological Modeling Conflict Theories.* Edison, NJ: Aldine Transaction Press.

Benson, P. L., Galbraith, J., & Espeland, P. (1998). *What Teens Need to Succeed.* Minneapolis, MN: Free Spirit Publishing.

Brownsword, A. (1987). *It Takes All Types.* Fairfax, CA: Baytree Publication.

Fairhurst, A. M., & Fairhurst, L. L.(1995). *Effective Teaching, Effective Learning.* Palo Alto, CA: Davis-Black Publishing.

Hammer, A. L., & Yeakley, F. R. (1987). The relationship between "true type" and reported type. *Journal of Psychological Type, 13,* 52–55.

Jackson, T. (2000). *Still More Activities that Teach.* Cedar City, UT: Red Rock Publishing.

Jakubowski-Spencer, P. (1973). *An Introduction to Assertive Training Procedures for Women.* Washington, DC: American Personnel and Guidance Association Press.

Keirsey, D., & Bates, M. (1998). *Please Understand Me II.* Del Mar, CA: Prometheus Nemesis Book Company.

Kroeger, O., Thuesen, J., & Rutledge, H. (2002). *Type Talk at Work (Revised).* New York: Random House.

Kummerow, J. A. (1988). A methodology for verifying type: research results. *Journal of Psychological Type, 15,* 20–25.

Kummerow, J., & Quenk, N. (2004). *Working with MBTI Step II Results*. Palo Alto, CA: CPP.

Lawrence, G., & Martin, C. (2001). *Building People, Building Programs*. Gainesville, FL: Center for Applications for Psychological Type.

Myers, I. B. (1993). *Introduction to Type* (5th ed.). Palo Alto, CA: Consulting Psychologists Press.

Myers, I. B., & Myers, P. B. (1980). *Gifts Differing*. Palo Alto, CA: Consulting Psychologists Press.

Myers, I. B., & McCaulley, M. H. (1985). *Manual: A Guide to the Development and Use of the Myers-Briggs Type Indicator*. Palo Alto, CA: Consulting Psychologist Press.

Oparah, D. (2006). *Make a World of Difference*. Minneapolis, MN: Search Institute.

Pearman, R. R., & Albirtton, S. C. (1997). *I'm Not Crazy, I'm Just Not You*. Palo Alto, CA: Davis-Black Publishing.

Ragsdale, S., & Saylor, A. (2007). *Great Group Games*. Minneapolis, MN: Search Institute.

Scales, P., & Liffert, N. (1999). *Developmental Assets*. Minneapolis, MN: Search Institute Press.

Sue, D., & Sue, D. (2007). *Foundations of Counseling and Psychotherapy: Evidence Based Practice for a Diverse Society*. New York: Wiley.

Tieger, P. D., Barron-Gieger, B. (2000). *Just Your Type*. New York: Little, Brown & Company.

Tindall, J. (2008). *Peer Power, Book One: Becoming an Effective Peer Helper and Conflict Mediator*. Boca Raton, FL: Taylor & Francis.

Tindall, J., & Black, D. R. (2008). *Peer Programs: An In-Depth Look at Peer Programs: Planning, Implementation, and Administration*. Boca Raton, FL: Taylor & Francis.

Tindall, J., Routson, S., & Lewis, P. (2003). A follow-up study of PICT peer helpers from 1986-93. *Peer Facilitator Quarterly, 19*, 72–79.

Tindall, J., & Salmon-White, S. (1990). *Peers Helping Peers: Program for the Preadolescent*. Muncie, IN: Accelerated Development.

Tindall, J., & Salmon, S. (1993). *Feelings: The 3 Rs—Receiving, Reflecting, Responding*. Muncie, IN: Accelerated Development.

VanSant, S. (2003). *Wired for Conflict: The Role of Personality in Resolving Differences*. Gainesville, FL: Center for Psychological Type.

Varenhorst, B. (2003). *An Asset Building Guide to Training Peer Helpers*. Minneapolis, MN: Search Institute Press.

Walck, C. (1992). The relationship between indicator type and "true type," slight preferences and the verification process. *Jounal of Psychological Type, 15*, 17–22.

Williams, S. R., & Bicknell-Behr, J. (1992). Assertiveness and psychological type. *Journal of Psychological Type, 23*, 27–37.

Zeissett, C. (2006). *The Art of Dialogue*. Gainesville, FL: Center for Applications of Psychological Type.

AUTHOR

Judith A. Tindall, PhD

Judith A. Tindall, PhD, is president of Psychological Network, Inc., a full-service psychological group in St. Charles, Missouri. She is currently licensed as a psychologist and professional counselor. She holds certifications as a teacher, school counselor, National Association of Peer Programs (NAPP) trainer/ consultant, Certified Peer Program Educator, Myers–Briggs Type Inventory (MBTI®)-certified trainer, and custody evaluator. She has been in private practice in St. Charles since the late 1970s. She has been a consultant at the local, state, national, and international level for both public and private organizations, associations, hospitals, schools, social service agencies, and the faith community. She has assisted those organizations on a wide variety of topics, including peer programs, safety, strategic planning, team building, leadership development, executive coaching, communication skills, care for the caregiver, total quality management, stress management, violence prevention, sexual harassment, diversity and MBTI®, community-building, HIV-AIDS, compulsive gambling, and other topics.

She has recently been elected vice president of the National Organizations for Youth Safety (NOYS), which is a collaborative organization made up of 40 youth-serving organizations. She also serves on the board of directors of NAPP, BACCHUS Peer Education Network, services for higher education, advocating for health and safety.

Some recent highlights of her work with peer programs are working with the National Highway Traffic Safety Administration (NHTSA) in evaluating projects on zero tolerance for underage drinking and driving and bike safety; helping the Future Farmers of America in creating a national evaluation model for its programs; consulting with the United Nations to develop and implement an international peer program and crisis management program (staff outreach support providers); and working with the Department of Education in Indiana and with Kansas City public schools regarding creating, enhancing, and evaluating peer programs. She currently leads her group in providing mental health services to St. Louis Job Corps. She has trained and consulted with thousands of adults internationally in a variety of peer programs and trained over 20,000 youth and adults in peer-delivered activities such as peer helping, mediation, leadership, tutoring, crisis management, traffic safety, health, and group work.

Prior to this, she worked in public schools for 18 years as a teacher, counselor, and guidance director. She has taught courses at the graduate level at the University of Missouri-St. Louis, Webster University, and Lindenwood University. Those courses included group process, assessment, of the individual, multicultural counseling, and other courses. Typical of her ENTJ (MBTI®), she has been an officer in local, state, and national professional organizations and volunteer organizations. She is past president of St. Charles Sunrise Rotary, National Peace Institute, National Peer Helpers Association, Missouri Peer Helpers Association, and Missouri Counselors Association; secretary for St. Louis Psychological Association; and vice president of the American School Counselors Association. She has received various recognitions from professional associations such as the National Peer Helpers Association Scholar of the Year and the Barbara Varenhorst Award of Merit, Missouri Counselors Association (MCA) distinguished service award, Harry S. Duncan Missouri Peer Helpers Assocation (MPHA) award, Missouri Mental Health

Counselors Association (MMHCA) association merit award, and St. Charles Sunrise Rotarian of the Year.

She has written many books: *Peer Program: An In-Depth Look at Peer Programs: Planning, Implementation, and Administration; Peer Power, Book One, Strategies for the Professional Leader: Becoming an Effective Peer Helper and Conflict Mediator; Peer Power, Book One, Workbook: Becoming an Effective Peer Helper and Conflict Mediator; Peer Power, Book Two, Strategies for the Professional Leader: Applying Peer Helper Skills; Peer Power, Book Two, Workbook: Applying Peer Helper Skills; Peers Helping Peers: Program for the Preadolescent and Leader's Manual; and Feelings: The 3 Rs—Receiving, Reflecting, Responding.* She has written many referred journal articles and for the popular press, including *St. Louis Busniess Journal* and *St. Charles Business Magazine.* She has also appeared on radio and television, including Good Morning America.

Dr. Tindall has a PhD in psychology from St. Louis University; Specialist from Southern Illinois University, Edwardsville in counseling and psychology; MEd from University of Missouri at Columbia; and a BS in education from Southwest Minnesota State University in Speech and Political Science. She is married, has two sons, and enjoys playing golf, spending time with friends, and reading. She is also a St. Louis Cardinals and St. Louis University Billikens fan.